A Story of
Vision and Values

*Memoirs of
DePauw University's
18th President*

Robert G. Bottoms
*President Emeritus
DePauw University*

TABLE OF CONTENTS

I want to dedicate this effort to Gwen,

my wife of over 50 years,

without whom I could not have

done what I have done.

Similarly, much of the success

I have achieved could never

have been possible without

the privilege of serving DePauw University

and having the support of the

many trustees and thousands of alumni.

PREFACE

AS I THINK BACK OVER MY CAREER I WANT TO KNOW HOW I BECAME THE PERSON THAT I AM. What did I learn from my experiences? Could this knowledge be helpful to someone else? I thought of writing a book on leadership, but the leadership field is already filled with books, mostly of questionable value. So I am on to this project, a sort of memoir, a sharing of my reflections on what I learned in my work spanning over five decades.

In the following pages I will tell my story. It chronicles a career seldom expected from a boy from Sandusky, Alabama. I have been very fortunate. I was in school with many friends brighter than I, but I received numerous breaks and unexpected opportunities. To be certain I made mistakes, but I did succeed in some things. My reflections will concentrate on lessons learned from successes. Chapter One focuses on my experiences growing up, the people who influenced me, my experience at the University of Virginia, my decision to become a Methodist minister, and my education at Birmingham Southern College, Emory University, and Vanderbilt University. Chapter Two discusses my twenty-two years as president of DePauw University and details many of the significant moments of my presidency. Chapter Three examines the decision making process I used as an administrator and serves as a guide to understand how decisions are made. Chapter Four reflects on the role that religion has played in my life. Finally,

Chapter Five discusses what I have learned about leadership in my various roles, not so much in theory, but more in "on the ground" experiences. My hopes for this book are twofold: I want our grandchildren to understand the values that informed my career, and I hope that other readers of these chapters might learn something about leadership.

I discovered in writing these memoirs that a life review can be exhausting. There were times my remembrances were joyful, and there were times my recollections made me sad. And there were days when I was tempted to abandon the whole project. Too many details to track down and too many temptations to omit portions of my story that might offend some of the people who worked alongside me. But I persevered much to the credit of John Dittmer, Emeritus Professor of History at DePauw, and a friend of many decades. John was not only a first-rate editor, but he also served as an insightful critic. I also want to thank Ken Owen, who was the Director of Public Relations for many of the years I was president of the university. It was Ken who researched the press accounts of the many controversies I faced at DePauw.

CHAPTER ONE

THE EARLY YEARS

I WAS BORN IN BIRMINGHAM, ALABAMA AND LIVED THE FIRST 18 YEARS OF MY LIFE WITH MY FATHER, MOTHER AND YOUNGER SISTER IN SANDUSKY, A SMALL SUBURB OF WHITE, MIDDLE-CLASS WORKING PEOPLE. Most everyone went to church, and the Methodist Church was central to our lives, both socially and spiritually. I was surrounded by caring people. My paternal grandparents lived two miles up the road from our house, adjacent to Sandusky School, which I attended. I walked to school each day, leaving home early enough to have breakfast with my grandparents-usually oatmeal and orange juice. I also spent a lot of time with my mother's parents who lived about four miles down the road. They frequently took me shopping on Saturdays in Birmingham's finest department stores, followed by lunch in Britlings Cafeteria, a big delight for me through my childhood.

Throughout grade school I was quite popular with my fellow students. I was also a favorite with my teachers, as I excelled in the classroom. No one my age lived close to me, and so after school was out there was no one to play with. I made up for the lack of playmates by reading a lot, mostly about sports. I had a vivid imagination, but no athletic ability. I was on the local baseball team but I seldom got into the game, and that was fine with me. I knew that if I batted I would probably strike out, and when I was in the field I spent most of my time hoping the ball would not be hit to me because my fielding was prone to errors.

By the time I was 14, I was old enough to cut grass. I had numerous yards to cut and this absorbed most of my free time. Not only did I cut grass, I also painted a lot, especially the kitchen cabinets for the many widows in the community. These odd jobs allowed me to make enough money to buy my own clothes and dress like the other kids.

There were no public swimming pools in Sandusky so I never learned to swim. I never learned to sing either. In fact, while in the Honor Society Choir in high school, the Music Director suggested that I just mouth the words rather than be heard singing off-key. I also never learned to dance as I had no sense of rhythm. But all was not lost. I found my niche on the debate team, won the state high school after dinner speaking contest and had significant roles in several plays. Because of my speaking ability, most of my classmates thought I was extroverted. However, I was quite shy around girls, and so I did not date much. I was a skinny 125 pounds and pretty self-conscious. I did not believe any girls would want to go out with me. This perception remained with me through my first-year of college at the University of Virginia. Given that the university was an all-male institution, any interaction with women was limited. We only met girls when they were bused in from surrounding women's colleges. Not much social life there.

This all changed in the summer of 1963. A friend gave a party for a dozen or so friends who were high school students and some who had come home from the first year of college. It was there that I met Gwen Vickers, the prettiest girl at the party. She was quite striking, with blonde hair and a blue madras blouse. The hostess of the party encouraged me to ask Gwen for a date. I did and this started a courtship that lasted five years. Finally I saved enough money to buy her a $500 engagement ring, and we were married in 1968 just after she graduated from Auburn University. Today, after 52 years of marriage, the romance lives on.

Growing up, three men in my family had a significant influence on me. The first was my father, Dalton Bottoms. He was a good man who was small in stature, having suffered from polio as a child. As a result his right arm was smaller than his left and his chest was smaller on the right side, almost as if someone had drawn a line through the middle of his body and diminished the right side by one half. Denied entrance into the army as a result of this condition, he worked in a factory in Baltimore supporting the war effort. He met my mother, they fell in love, they were married and decided to live in Birmingham. Through the influence of his father, the superintendent of a small local post office, my dad secured a position as a rural letter carrier, a position he held until his death in 1972.

My father never went to college, but he was a very intelligent man. He was industrious and could build or fix almost anything, a talent he used to supplement his income from the post office to make a better life for his family. He built the small concrete block house I lived in as a child. As his income increased from various projects, he added a den to our house and later two additional bedrooms, as well as a screen porch and carport. He financed these additions from the income he made as a small contractor, adding rooms to the houses of people in our community. He also used the land of his father-in-law to plant several acres of watermelons, which he sold from a trailer pulled behind his car through the mostly black communities where he carried the mail.

When some of my friends purchased motorbikes from Sears and Roebuck for over $100, my father bought an old whizzer bike from a neighbor for $15. Initially it would not run at all, but my father fixed it and soon I had the fastest motorbike in the community. I had a similar experience when go-karts became popular. Not able to afford the expensive ones, my dad built one from scratch and we made a dirt racetrack in the backyard just beyond the clothesline. It was a place where I could win races against my friends with the fancier models. These are all pleasant memories, but there was another aspect to my relationship with my dad. Three memories stand out.

My dad was proud of the free-standing workshop he built in the back of our house. I watched with envy as he made things either for our house or to sell to neighbors. He was especially good at making coffee tables. At six years of age I wanted to try my hand at making something and I needed to use his hatchet to do so. He initially said I was not old enough to use the hatchet, but I begged so long that he relented. I went outside the workshop to cut a piece of wood, and to my embarrassment, I cut my left hand pretty bad. There was no way to hide the mistake as the wound was deep and quite bloody. I showed my dad who said I had done exactly what he was afraid of, and we were off to the doctor. It took 23 stitches to sew me up, and at 76 years of age I can still see the scar. It was the beginning of my feeling that I could really disappoint my father.

That same year I developed a viral infection. We visited the elderly Dr. Cloud in Ensley, Alabama, who decided he needed a urine sample. This was a new experience for me. He gave me a small cup, sent me into a room, closed the door and told me to come out when I filled the cup. A few minutes passed and the door opened. The small cup was sitting on the floor empty. My pants were unzipped and I was holding my penis in my hand. The doctor laughed and my dad laughed even harder. Only then was I told to hold the cup in one hand and my penis in the other! I had to listen to my dad tell this story over and over, and this hurt me. No one likes to be laughed at, and this incident was a second reminder that I was capable of falling short of expectations.

At age 15 I received my learner's permit to drive a car, and my father decided he should teach me. He had a blue-and-white 1955 Chevrolet that was very impressive to a young driver. Things went well at first, as the many years of driving my go-kart served as good preparation. At least I had knowledge of steering and braking. Then one day, when my father was adding a room onto my grandfather's house, the Chevrolet needed to be backed up in the driveway. My dad asked if I would like to do it by myself. The driveway was straight and flat. It was my first time alone in the car and I readily agreed. It was not like driving on the street but it was a start and 30 yards did not seem like much of a challenge. I started the car, raced the engine and put it in reverse. My father came off the construction project and raced down the drive yelling at me, "Don't you ever do that again! You can ruin a car by putting it in gear with the engine running so fast." I had never seen my father so angry. Furthermore, at age 15, I could not ever remember anyone yelling at me. I burst into tears and replied that I never wanted to drive again. Never. Of course, I did drive again but 60 years later I can still recall my feelings of complete failure. Just another reminder that I had the ability to disappoint others.

From these experiences you can see I had mixed interactions with my dad. I admired his ability to create things and his hard work to provide a good life for the family. I so wanted to please him, but I found this difficult because he sometimes made me feel inadequate.

The most significant person for me growing up was my maternal grandfather, Robert Cruce. Even though he was my grandfather he always wanted me to call him "Bob," a tradition still present in our family as I too have my grandchildren call me by my first name, as opposed to "grandfather." Bob was a supervisor in a small rail yard that belonged to the Tennessee Coal and Iron Company (TCI). While he, like others in my family, had no college education, he was a wise man. One of the things that pleased him most was that when he retired it took three men to fill his job, all of whom had degrees from Georgia Tech. Bob earned the best salary of anyone in the family. He was the first to own a television and the first to have an electric razor. While he was not one to boast, he always dressed well and drove nice cars. His pride was a 1960 brown-and-white Bonneville Pontiac with a large V8 engine. Shortly after purchasing the car he and my grandmother planned a trip to California. He recruited me to go along to help him drive…a tremendous vote of confidence for a young inexperienced driver.

Bob always had some discretionary income and he kept at least $100 in his wallet at all times, a lot of money in the 1950's. He gave me a dollar for every "A" I made on my report card and paid me well for cutting his grass. In the summer heat he would frequently finish the lawn himself, not wanting me to get too hot. When I was preparing to leave for my first year of college at the University of Virginia, Bob learned that all the students wore coats and ties, so he took me to one of the nicest department stores in Birmingham and bought me an expensive green gabardine suit and a fine wool overcoat. None of us knew at the time that the UVA students dressed in khaki pants, blue shirts and navy blazers. How I stood out attending my first fraternity party dressed in my nice gabardine suit, the strange boy from Sandusky, Alabama!

My mother's brother, Jack Cruce, also had a profound impact on me. Like Bob and my father, Uncle Jack had no college education. He was a tail gunner in the Navy during the war and after he returned home, he lived with my grandmother and Bob. My grandmother used to complain that Jack stayed out too late and possibly drank too much. After he married he settled down and, to my knowledge, never drank again. He, Bob and my father built the house he and his wife, Joyce, lived in until he died.

Jack spent a substantial amount of time with me before I went off to college. When I was a child he built a wagon for me that was much faster than the soap box derby models, and I raced it down the long hill that was our driveway. He also took me hunting and gave me the only rifle I ever owned…a single shot .22 caliber rifle that had belonged to him as a boy. He was quite imaginative with the games we played. I remember one time in particular. He asked if I was willing to use a parachute if he made one for me, and of course I answered yes. So he made me a parachute out of an old sheet with appropriate strings attached to each of the four corners and empty spools of thread as the handles. He used a ladder to place me on the top of Bob's garage and was about to let me jump off until my grandmother saw what was happening and came out the door screaming, "Jack, you will kill that boy if you do not stop your shenanigans with him." That ended my paratrooper training, and even though Jack was willing to let me jump, I was no worse for the wear and tear from all our times together.

Jack was an electrician with TCI. He retired early and fished a lot. Jack also spent a great deal of time watching stock car races on television and sitting on his back porch smoking cigarettes and drinking coffee. He seldom used the red pickup truck that he loved, except to go fishing or hunting. When I grew up he was always glad to see me when I came to visit. He treated me as though my visits were special. Jack was at peace with himself and in my retirement I think of him often. Like Jack I do not care much for travel, I do enjoy my cigars and I basically like to sit outside and be left alone. The only exception to being left alone was that Jack liked to spend time with his children and grandchildren and so do I. Growing up with my dad, Bob and Jack provided me with many memories.

While my dad, Bob, and Jack had a significant influence on me growing up, there were two women who also need to be mentioned. One was my maternal grandmother affectionately called "Granny." If Bob made me feel special, Granny was not far behind. While Bob and Granny had four grandchildren, I was the only grandson. Granny loved all of her grandchildren, but she viewed me as special. At Christmas, after all of the presents were opened, she would motion for me to meet her in the back bedroom of her house where she would slip me money, sometimes as much as $100. She rationalized this behavior because she said, "Boys just need more than girls."

Granny was always present when Bob took me shopping, and it was at her suggestion that we only shop the best brands. After I became a minister, Granny was especially proud, and she frequently came to hear me preach. Even though no one in our family spoke out against segregation, Granny once confided in me that perhaps Martin Luther King was right in promoting racial equality, although she certainly never mentioned this to anyone else in the family.

My mother, Inez Bottoms, also made me feel special. This showed in the meals she prepared for the family dinner. The menu usually consisted of my favorite foods: fried fish, fried chicken, fried oysters and fried pork chops. I never had meat that was not fried until I was off to college. Mother taught grammar school during several of my childhood years. Even though she had only gone to college for one year, she was able to secure a teaching position in an elementary school because her uncle was the local school principal, and in the 1950's no college degree was required to teach in Alabama. Looking back, I imagine she was a good teacher. She loved the children in her class, and she was diligent about correcting papers every night.

Mother sacrificed a lot to give me what I wanted. My father always drove Chrysler products on his rural mail route, but Mother was the proud owner of a white 1960 Chevrolet Impala with a red interior. When I was about to begin my sophomore year at Birmingham Southern College, Dad thought I should have a car.

I had earned enough money at various odd jobs to buy a used car, but my father thought I should have a new one. He located a white 1964 Chevrolet Impala Super Sport with red bucket seats, and so he took my mother's car and the money I had saved to make the purchase possible. Mother never complained about giving up her car for me. Just another piece of evidence that in my family being a male, and in my case a minister, was indeed special.

Because I made excellent grades in school, I won a scholarship to the School of Engineering at the University of Virginia. My father and mother drove me to Charlottesville in the fall of 1962. Arriving at the all-male institution where students wore coats and ties was quite impressive, to say nothing of the beautiful grounds. But it took only a few weeks for me to realize two things. The first was that I was not cut out to be an engineer. The second was that my education in the Birmingham public school system had not prepared me for the rigors of the university. From day one I was behind in all my science courses. I took physics with a lab, chemistry with a lab and calculus. I studied hard, but almost everything was over my head. Confronted with academic failure for the first time in my life, I began to search for a new pathway. I grew up in church and was a regular attendee at the University Baptist Church in Charlottesville. One Sunday evening the pastor preached a sermon on how God needed young men to become ministers. I thought maybe this would be for me. I had always enjoyed church, and I was kind to people and a good speaker.

Becoming a minister would at least get me out of engineering.

When I announced to my family that I felt a calling to the ministry and wanted to transfer to Birmingham Southern College to begin the preparation to become a Methodist minister, everyone in my family was thrilled except my father. My announcement about a career change came about the same time my second semester grades arrived. I had not failed chemistry but I had come close. Holding my grade slip in his hand, my father disappointedly said to me, "This is not what we have sacrificed for."

I was devastated, for he believed that entering the ministry was an excuse for my poor grades at the UVA. Again I had fallen short of my father's expectation. However, when he heard me preach my first sermon at the Sandusky Methodist Church, he came to me with tears in his eyes and said that he had been wrong to be disappointed in me. He was now pleased that I wanted to prepare for the ministry.

When I arrived at Birmingham Southern everyone in my church was proud of me, especially my family. But something was wrong. At 19 years of age I had nothing to say. How could I even begin to prepare a sermon? I solved this dilemma by subscribing to a fundamentalist publication called *The Sword of the Lord*. Basically I plagiarized many of the sermons I read. R.T. Sanderson, our pastor at the time, called on me to preach regularly, and because of my speaking ability, I was an enormous success. I can recall one parishioner, who was a close friend of the family, saying, "God must have called him or else he could not preach like this." This remark cast the first ray of doubt about my new vocation because I knew that if I had not adopted the ideas of others I would have, in fact, been speechless.

But not all of my time was spent learning to preach. Before starting my sophomore year at Birmingham Southern I secured a job at Birmingham Rail and Locomotive, a small business that bought old railroads and cut up the iron rails to melt down so they could be used again. At age 19 I learned to use a blowtorch. The hours were long and the work was hard, but instructive, as all but one of my fellow laborers was black. Having spent his career in a rail yard, Bob knew how hot and challenging this summer job was. He offered to give me an equivalent amount of money if I would quit and find less dangerous employment, but I turned him down as I had begun to experience the freedom of being self-sufficient. I earned enough money at Birmingham Rail to pay my way through Birmingham Southern and purchase a white 1964 Chevrolet Impala Super Sport automobile with red bucket seats.

At age 19 I was appointed student pastor of the Pine Grove Methodist Church, a small congregation in rural Jefferson County close to the Warrior River. What I lacked in formal training I made up for by studying the sermons of others. I well remember my first funeral service. Aunt Emma Johnson, an elderly member of the church, had died. I was to plan and lead the funeral service. The church members were more nervous than I because they wanted me to do well but they knew how inexperienced I was. Thanks to the Methodist Order of Worship and a few ideas borrowed from others I was able to get through the service.

Then it was on to the cemetery for the burial. The August heat was oppressive and when we arrived at the cemetery I knew something was wrong. The grave diggers had done their work and left. But they had placed the vault on a pile of dirt, not in the grave as it was supposed to be. The grave was dug too small to accommodate the vault. Undaunted by this dilemma I took off my coat, grabbed a shovel and enlarged the grave to enable the vault to be placed inside. Coatless and covered with sweat I concluded the service. I was the nineteen-year-old hero of Pine Grove Church. This, coupled with the fact that I organized and led the painting of the church basement, taught me a lesson. The combination of hard work and a good speaking voice can go a long way in the Methodist Church.

My days at Birmingham Southern were happy ones. I continued to pastor the Pine Grove Church and I became a senior counselor and guest preacher at Camp Sumatanga, the camp for the youth of the North Alabama Conference. It was a nice recognition and I thoroughly enjoyed speaking before hundreds of young people. At Birmingham Southern I took classes with Dr. J. Maxwell Miller, a freshly-minted Professor of Old Testament from the Candler School of Theology at Emory University. He was the first person I ever knew who took the higher criticism of the Bible seriously. His courses began to open my eyes to what might lie ahead in my graduate study at Emory.

After finishing college I entered the Candler School of Theology at Emory, much to the dismay of some of my parents' friends. One man in particular, Ramsey Hayes, warned my dad and me that Emory would ruin my faith. Mr. Hayes tried to persuade me to attend Asbury Theological School in Wilmore, Kentucky, a fundamentalist institution. Nonetheless, I decided to attend Emory, but I must admit Mr. Hayes was partially right. It was not so much that Emory undercut my faith as it exposed my naiveté and began to give meaning to a faith informed as much by reason as by emotion. I read liberal theologians like Rudolf Bultmann, Paul Tillich and Dietrich Bonhoeffer, and I became serious about my studies for the first time. I excelled in the classroom and marveled at my ability to address both academics and life's significant questions at the same time. It was during my first year at Emory that it dawned on me that God may not have called me into the ministry at all. Perhaps I was just so depressed at the University of Virginia that the ministry looked good to me. It was an emotional choice soon to be overcome by the growth of my intellect.

My days at Emory were interesting ones. The Candler School of Theology in the 1960's did not have the high academic standing that it enjoys today. Almost all the students were Methodists and many pastored churches on the weekend. For that reason there were no Monday classes so students could have the day to travel back to school. Also, most of the students were men, as few women were encouraged to become ordained ministers. Our women classmates at Candler planned to become Directors of Christian Education...a real commentary on the Southern church at that time. Men could become pastors and lead the churches while women could become DCEs (Directors of Christian Education) and manage the Sunday Schools.

While there were only a few women enrolled in Candler there was no black presence. In fact, I can recall only one black student in the entire student body. Clearly, in my day, Candler was a school that primarily existed to produce white male clergy for the Methodist church. Nonetheless, the seeds of change were beginning to take place as some faculty began to focus on racial injustice in the South. And Atlanta was an interesting place to house the School of Theology. Atlanta was moderately progressive as Southern cities of that time went. I can still recall a column published by Ralph McGill in *The Atlanta Constitution* where he told the story of a white first grader talking to his mother. The boy was attending a newly integrated school and it came to the mother's attention that one of her son's best friends, Johnny I believe was his name, was black. The white mother quizzed her son about his newfound friend to see if there was anything "different" about him. Finally she asked, "Is Johnny a Negro?" Her son replied, "I don't know. I will ask him." Now, some 50 years later, I can still remember this column and the impact it had on my developing idealism.

During my first year at Candler, I worked in the library during the day and unloaded packages at United Parcel at night. Then, on the weekend, I served as the Assistant Pastor of the North Decatur Methodist Church. Before I began my second year in seminary I was appointed the student pastor of the Glenn Hills Methodist Church in Bessemer, Alabama, and so I joined the ranks of Candler students who commuted back and forth between school and church. In June, before I entered my third and final year at Candler, Gwen and I were married. My salary at Glenn Hills was too modest to support us, and we decided Gwen should get a job in Atlanta. We were down to our last $100 before she was hired as a home economist for the Atlanta Gaslight Company. Gwen worked 40 hours a week and we left Atlanta on Friday evening for the 120 mile drive to the parsonage in Bessemer. We returned to our apartment in Atlanta on Sunday evening after church. To say that this was an adventuresome first year of marriage would be an understatement.

After graduating from Candler I became pastor of the Friendship United Methodist Church in Athens, Alabama. Athens was a small county seat town in Northern Alabama. Many of the townspeople were farmers, but Athens was only about 30 miles from Huntsville, and some of the parishioners worked in the space industry at Redstone Arsenal. We had a congregation of about 200 well-educated people who were always gracious to Gwen and me.

My salary at the church was $6,000 and Gwen taught first grade to supplement our income. Adding to the significance of our time in Athens, Gwen gave birth to our son, David, in August, 1970.

While pastoring Friendship Church two events happened that illustrate how deeply ingrained segregation was in Alabama. When Gwen was assigned her first grade teaching slot in a rural Limestone County school, she discovered that, while the school was integrated, a Mrs. Ryan, who was a member of our church, had an all-white class and all the black children were in Gwen's class. These black children were mostly from low-income families and had little formal training. Upon Gwen's suggestion we started a preschool program at our church to help prepare black children for first grade. A reporter from the local paper learned of the kindergarten at Friendship and asked if he could write a story about it. I thought this would be good publicity for the church, but when the pictures came out in the paper showing our white parishioners teaching black children in a county where no blacks attended a white church, many townspeople were upset. I even received a telephone call from the minister of the First Methodist Church in town. He wanted to inquire as to what exactly we were up to, and he cautioned me not to promote the integration of blacks and whites. Our church, however, was quite proud of the program. I had innocently touched a nerve in Limestone County.

Another interesting thing happened in 1971. John Cashin, a black dentist from Huntsville, was running for governor against

George Wallace, the staunch segregationist. It just so happened that this was the first election where voting machines rather than paper ballots were used in the county. Of course, George Wallace defeated Cashin easily. The day after the election I went into town to get a haircut. Several men were already in the barbershop, and they were discussing the election. They were none too happy about the new voting machines. They felt people were either confused by the machines or the machines had incorrectly tabulated the votes. The evidence for their belief was that two votes had been cast for Cashin in an all-white precinct. I kept my mouth shut, not wanting at that particular time to divulge that those two votes were not in error. They had been cast by Gwen and me!

During my first year at Friendship I learned of the Doctor of Ministry program at Vanderbilt University. I investigated the program for two reasons. The first was that Wilhelm Pauck was on the faculty. Dr. Pauck had been a friend and colleague of Paul Tillich when they both taught at Union Theological Seminary in New York. Throughout my time at Emory, Tillich had been the theologian whose writings had most influenced me, and going to Vanderbilt would be a chance to pursue my understanding of Tillich with a man who knew him personally. My second reason was less noble. Having a doctoral degree appealed to my ego, to be known as Dr. Bottoms rather than Reverend Bottoms. Vanderbilt was but a two hour drive from Athens, and my course work could be taken on Tuesdays and Thursdays. The church agreed to let me pursue the degree while still serving as pastor. Accepted into the program, I completed the two years of residence work at Vanderbilt while in Athens. These two years proved to be the most challenging and educationally fulfilling experiences of my career. I was able to study with Dr. Pauck and his course on John Calvin was one of the highlights of my time at Vanderbilt. Dr. Pauck also oversaw my D.Min. thesis entitled "The Practical Implications of Paul Tillich's Theology for a Doctrine of Church Renewal." I was further challenged by other faculty who remained friends for decades.

After completing my two years at Vanderbilt we moved to Birmingham, Alabama in 1971. I became the Associate Pastor of the First United Methodist Church, a large and thriving downtown church whose ministry centered on preaching. My responsibilities were to visit the hospitals, teach a young adults Sunday School Class, and preach on Sunday evening. The third task was the most enjoyable, because several hundred people came to hear me speak every week from this historic pulpit. During my first year in Birmingham I completed my thesis at Vanderbilt and became Dr. Bottoms.

I was off to a good start as a Methodist minister, but two things happened that became formative in my career. The first was a proposal for First Methodist Church to begin a preschool program. Such a program would not only utilize our educational facilities, which were empty during the week, but would also serve the needs of young parents who worked downtown and needed quality childcare. In the beginning I was not very interested in the project, choosing instead to concentrate on my preaching. Yet the proposal became controversial, and I was drawn into the conflict. Those who opposed the project did so on racial grounds. What if black parents wanted their children to enroll? A hotly contested debate ensued. If, in fact, we were followers of the gospel that I preached each Sunday night how could we deny black children the opportunity to use our facilities? The answer was clear to me. The black children should be welcomed, but this posed a problem for many. Some of the very people who praised my preaching were firmly against allowing blacks to enroll in the kindergarten. It *was the first time I realized that behavior does not always follow the spoken word.* To say the least I was disheartened, and I began to question whether my preaching had any positive effect at all.

That same year another development caused me to question my profession. My father, who had been diagnosed with lung cancer just prior to my first year in Birmingham, died. His last days were filled with excruciating pain, and his death had a profound influence on me. During the family time at the funeral home many religious folk came by to offer their condolences and share their interpretations of what death meant...that for Christians it was the passing into the heaven we had been taught about as children. In heaven we would be greeted by angels and reunited with loved ones who had preceded us in death. His death was the first in my family I experienced as an adult, and I had to admit to myself that intellectually I could not comprehend the traditional doctrine concerning heaven promoted by the conservative Southern church. Growing up in the Sandusky Methodist Church, believing in Jesus was a natural thing. All my teachers and pastors believed that the Bible was literally true. But now having been exposed to liberal theology and experiencing the death of my father, it was apparent that there was a disconnect between my doubts about the existence of an afterlife and what I was supposed to promote as a minister. Thus, between my disappointment with the church kindergarten debacle and facing the realization that I did not adhere to church doctrine, I had to confront the fact that at age 28 I was in a profession I could not remain in if I was intellectually honest with myself. But what was I to do?

The answer came unexpectedly. While wrestling with my dilemma I received a call from Ralph Tanner, the president of Birmingham Southern College. It just so happened that Donald Shockley, the college chaplain, had resigned to accept a position at the University of the Redlands in California. Ralph offered me the job. I met with him and explained that my career plans were in a state of flux, but that I was probably on my way out of the ministry, and I had no idea what I should do. Ralph said if I would just take the job we could figure out my next step together. In some ways this was a perfect solution. I had been honest with Ralph in telling him that I viewed the chaplaincy as a way to buy some time to decide on my future, and he accepted this. Now I had a prized position. I could be on a college campus that nurtured intellectual honesty and I was free to work with faculty who challenged me to grow.

My time as a college chaplain was enjoyable. Yeilding Chapel, where I preached and had my office, was beautiful. My major adjustment to college life was realizing most students couldn't have cared less whether the college had a chaplain or not. The numbers of students and faculty who came to the Sunday service were small. But this was all right with me because I had a lot of time to read and study, and with so much free time I could concentrate on being a good husband and father. The move to Birmingham Southern meant Gwen and I had to move out of a Methodist parsonage and buy a house of our own. Gwen's father loaned us the money for a down payment on our first house, and we were proud to have it. We spent a lot of time fixing it up, including adding a nursery for our second child, a daughter, Leslie, who was born in February, 1974.

I worked for a year as chaplain, and in 1973 the unexpected happened again. Larry Durham, the Director of Development at Southern, resigned and Ralph asked me to take the job. I did not know what "development" was, but serving as Ralph's assistant appealed to me. This was my first step away from the traditional work of the clergy. After a year in this job, Ralph decided to leave the presidency. I was too young and inexperienced to have the opportunity to replace Ralph. Amidst the uncertainty of who might be the next president, and whether or not I might even have a job, Joe Sparks, the Assistant Dean of Students at Southern, interviewed for the position of Assistant Dean of the Vanderbilt Divinity School. Joe, who was a close friend of mine, was offered the job but he turned it down because it entailed fundraising, a task he was not interested in. But Joe, when declining the job offer, recommended me. Sallie TeSelle, the first woman to be the dean of any divinity school in the country, invited me to Nashville for an interview. We hit it off well and I was offered the job. My role was to raise money, oversee the admissions program and teach one course on stewardship. It was the perfect transition from the clergy to university administrator. My years at the Divinity School were terrific.

At Vanderbilt I was surrounded by faculty I respected and grew to love. Gwen and I attended the Belle Meade Methodist Church and I occasionally preached in both Presbyterian and Disciples of Christ churches. Aside from my work in the church I enjoyed teaching my class on stewardship and leading the development program for the Divinity School. Before I arrived, the Divinity School had little in the way of an organized development program. The Lilly Endowment had initiated a program to assist seminaries across the country learn how to raise money by developing a professional staff. The Endowment recruited several development consultants to assist in this task and assigned them to various seminaries.

Robert E. Nelson, a consultant from Chicago, was designated for Vanderbilt, and he began to teach me the fundamentals of raising money. Bob Nelson was the perfect consultant for me. Unlike some development consultants, Bob had actually been a successful fundraiser at the Illinois Institute of Technology before becoming a consultant. Working with him, we cultivated Nashville business people by hosting a monthly breakfast at the school where we could showcase our work and potentially build a donor base of lay people.

I also taught a church school class at the Second Presbyterian Church that contained many prominent Vanderbilt alumni. Teaching the class was secondary. My primary motive was to promote what we were doing in the Divinity School. I was successful in showcasing our program and several of the Vanderbilt trustees who attended Second Presbyterian made unsolicited gifts to the school. I also developed some theological courses for lay people that I lead in the parishes of some of the Divinity School alumni. Slowly we interested many lay people in supporting the school. Because of these programs I was quite successful in raising money, but I became frustrated with the university policy which did not allow me to solicit alumni from other schools in the university even though they might be interested in the work of the divinity school. I was seriously considering leaving Vanderbilt because of this. My work was well enough known in theological circles that I was offered an Assistant Dean's position at the Yale Divinity School. I was almost seduced by Yale's reputation, but I realized that I would be faced by the same university policy at Yale that I disliked at Vanderbilt.

Having turned down the Yale position and continuing to be frustrated at Vanderbilt, I began to explore career opportunities at liberal arts colleges. Good fortune struck again. In 1978 I applied for the chief development position at DePauw University in Greencastle, Indiana, and I got the job, my first with no connection to the ministry after graduate school.

Because DePauw was a Methodist school, Gwen and I planned to attend the Methodist Church located on the corner of the campus. This turned out to be a mistake. The minister there was a complete irritant for me. The problem was that he was just like me during my early experiences in the Methodist Church. He was a gifted speaker but his sermons reminded me of what I used to say and had rebelled against. The church, as had been the case at the First Methodist Church in Birmingham, was pulpit-centered and I saw little evidence of the parish connecting what was said from the pulpit to the needs of our community. One Sunday after church I told Gwen I needed to leave the Methodist Church. We and the children visited several churches in Greencastle and settled on Saint Andrews Episcopal Church where we were confirmed. I turned in my clergy orders to the Methodist Church, effectively severing ties with the institution in which I had grown up. Ted Jones, the Episcopal Bishop of Indiana, learned of my seminary background and asked if I was interested in becoming an Episcopal priest. It was an interesting proposal, but I declined, thus making a final career choice to separate from the formal ministry. I became an active lay person in the Episcopal Church, serving as an Episcopal representative to the National Council of Churches (which most people in the Sandusky Methodist Church thought was a communist organization) and I was the Senior Warden of the local parish. One might say I had a love/hate relationship with the institutional church, but religion always played a significant role in my life.

When I decided to leave Vanderbilt Divinity School to take the secular position at DePauw most of my family was devastated since they could think of no higher calling than being a minister. My grandfather, Bob, on the other hand took me outside into his garage away from my mother and grandmother, who were crying about my decision. He said to me, "Don't worry about them. You are too smart to be a Methodist preacher." Keep in mind that this came from a devoted Methodist who seldom missed church and always made a large financial commitment. His comment did not reflect so much on the church as it underscored his confidence in me. He wanted to give me the courage to plan my own life. Certainly he was the greatest positive influence on my life, always loving and supporting me no matter what.

In 1978 we moved to Greencastle, Indiana. We purchased an old Victorian house close to the campus on Seminary Street. The children spent their early years there. Both David and Leslie had many friends, so the large old house was a beehive of activity. The children excelled in school and they were both active in sports. David played basketball and baseball, and Leslie played basketball and tennis. Each of the children also worked. David had a job at the local car wash and Leslie worked at the marina on Lake Monroe. With school, sports and work, the children were always busy. I worked long hours at the university, sometimes arriving at the office at 5:00 AM. Gwen also worked, first as the Director of Summer Programs at the university and later as Coordinator of Alumni Travel. When the Walden Inn was built on campus, Gwen served as the Director of Marketing. We were quite the active family.

At DePauw I was the Vice President for University Relations, and we hired Bob Nelson as our development consultant. With his help we completely overhauled the development office. We separated alumni affairs and the annual fund into two distinct functions, and we initiated a planned giving program. We also researched the giving history of the university. While the development program had been modest for several decades, one major gift stood out. In April of 1919, Edward Rector, an attorney from Chicago who had become interested in DePauw, announced he would provide enough money to establish 100 full tuition scholarships for male students annually in perpetuity. Rector's gift sharply distinguished DePauw from other colleges across the Midwest. While there is no definitive method for establishing the Rector gift in today's dollars, Lewis Gulick in his book, *An Investment in Humanity*, estimates that the gift to be worth in excess of $100 million dollars today.

At its peak there were 400 Rector Scholars on campus at one time. These men (Women were included later.) had been valedictorians and salutatorians of their high school classes. They graduated from the university and became successful entrepreneurs, CEOs and leaders in their communities. What we discovered was that they had never been aggressively solicited for a gift to DePauw. We surveyed the 3,000 living Rector Scholars and found that they had warm feelings toward the university. With this group as our foundation we began the Sesquicentennial Campaign, which raised over $120 million dollars and at that time (1987) was the largest amount of money any liberal arts college in the United States had ever raised.

⌐

CHAPTER TWO

BECOMING A UNIVERSITY PRESIDENT

HAVING THE OPPORTUNITY TO LEAD THE SESQUICENTENNIAL CAMPAIGN GAVE ME THE CHANCE TO GET TO KNOW ALL MEMBERS OF THE BOARD OF TRUSTEES VERY WELL. We worked closely together and Dick Rosser, the DePauw president at the time, spoke highly of me to the Board. In fact, Dick often referred to me as his alter ego. There were almost no important decisions made by Rosser that were not thoroughly discussed with me. In the fall of 1985, Dick was granted a sabbatical and I was named Acting President for the 1985-86 school year. I viewed my task to be a placeholder on the academic side, and to use my talents mostly in development to complete the Sesquicentennial Campaign. However a tension between the faculty and the administration interfered with my rather simplistic view of my challenge. Let me explain.

Before Dick Rosser left on sabbatical, large numbers of faculty developed a belief that Dick allowed some members of the community to influence his tenure and promotion decisions outside the normal channels of the Committee on Faculty. To my surprise, at the September, 1985 faculty meeting, my first as Acting President, the faculty voted not to participate in the personnel process until the veil of secrecy was removed. I had two choices. I could just go it alone as the Acting President and make tenure and promotion decisions without faculty input or I could attempt to work out a new and open process acceptable to the faculty. Under pressure, I chose the second alternative.

The faculty elected a small group to work with me and the Academic Vice President to address the perceived secrecy. We worked throughout the fall semester and arrived at a new process. It was decided that the president should make decisions on tenure and promotion solely on information in the candidate's written file. This meant we had moved to what was called an "open file" process and the candidate could see everything in his or her file, i.e. the departmental recommendation, the Committee on Faculty recommendation and the recommendation of the Academic Vice President. If any faculty member outside the department or the Committee of Faculty wanted to file a minority report, or an individual report for that matter, they had to submit their view in writing and the candidate had a right to respond. The faculty approved this process and to my knowledge the open file process exists to this day.

Having this contentious work behind me and with the continuing progress of the Sesquicentennial Campaign, I was ready for my second semester as Acting President. Again the unexpected happened. In January, 1986, Bob Frederick, the incoming Chair of the Board of Trustees, came into my office and told me that Dick Rosser had resigned and that the Executive Committee of the Board of Trustees wanted to make me the president. I was flabbergasted. I had received no signal that Dick had planned on leaving the presidency, and I had no idea how the faculty might react to such a change. I proposed to the trustees that they work with a duly elected faculty committee to examine three options: conduct a national search for a new president and not have me as a candidate, conduct a national search and have me as a candidate, or have no national search and name me the president.

The faculty committee consulted with the trustees throughout January and came to the conclusion that I be named the 18th president of DePauw, a decision that I believe was based on our fundraising success and my ability to work with the faculty to develop a personnel process acceptable to both the faculty and administration. My inauguration was set for October and Alexander Heard, the Chancellor of Vanderbilt University and my former mentor, was the keynote speaker. A second speaker, Professor Arthur Carkeek of the School of Music represented the faculty. Professor Carkeek, an Episcopalian himself, began his remarks by saying that he never, and he meant *never*, expected DePauw to have an Episcopalian as president. The seventeen former presidents of the university had all been Methodists, and all but one had been Methodist clergy.

So, how does one learn to be president of a college? To be sure I had observed and learned from Ralph Tanner at Birmingham Southern (See Appendix I), Alexander Heard at Vanderbilt and

Dick Rosser at DePauw. I thought I was well prepared, but I soon discovered that actually sitting in the chair of the president is quite different and more challenging than sitting outside and observing.

Bob Nelson proved to be an important mentor. I also developed friendships with other college presidents. George Harmon of Millsaps College taught me that as a college president your friends come and go, but your enemies accumulate. Michelle Myers of Denison University was a model of how one might deal with a Greek system. Henry Copeland of the College of Wooster showed me how to remain graceful in the face of public criticism, and Nancy Dye of Oberlin College was a person who, when faced with financial challenges, was always transparent and truthful. I learned a lot from these trusted colleagues.

The Campaign for DePauw was the second major fundraising campaign for the university, and it was begun in the early days of my presidency. It, too, was quite successful and enabled us to raise DePauw's stature as a national liberal arts college. In the fundraising arena I was most interested in securing funds for scholarships and faculty development. While significant money was raised for scholarships we were also able to endow 38 faculty chairs, which allowed us to increase faculty salaries so as to be competitive with our peer institutions. But we also had to address many building needs. We were so successful that, twenty years into my presidency, Tim Ubben, the Chair of the Board of Trustees at the time, called me "Bob the Builder." During my time as president we built the Olin Biological Sciences Building, the Pulliam Center for Contemporary Media, the Manning Environmental Field Station, the Ian and Mimi Rowland Welcome Center, the Janet Prindle Ethics Institute, the Bartlett Reflection Center, the Peeler Art Center, Humbert Hall, and Rector Village. We also renovated the Julian Math and Science Center, the Emison Art Center, and the Judson and Joyce Green Center for the Performing Arts. All told we raised $190 million for these projects.

As a result of the Campaign for DePauw, the endowment grew from $83 million to over $550 million. This success was attributable to two factors. First, the Phillip Holton estate was settled and DePauw was the beneficiary of a $122 million bequest. While Holton had attended DePauw for only one year before transferring to the School of Engineering at Purdue University, he had met his wife, Ruth, at DePauw and he always considered DePauw "his school." Second, when the news of the Holton bequest became known, we had begun a financial campaign with a goal of $160 million. The Board of Trustees wisely decided not to declare victory as a result of the Holton gift, but to raise our goal to $375 million. The Holton gift was important not only for the University's balance sheet, but psychologically it allowed us to overcome what I had felt was an inferiority complex when we compared ourselves to the best liberal arts colleges in the country. Now, with such a large influx of funds, we could dream of new levels of excellence. When the Campaign for DePauw concluded we had raised $392 million and this set a record for private liberal arts colleges. Thus the groundwork was laid for the many changes that needed to be made at DePauw.

How did all of this happen? We had scores of gifted people in the development office and they worked hard, but the real key to our success was the loyal alumni body as literally thousands of them supported our campaign. Alumni gave out of appreciation for what DePauw had meant for them, and their desire to positively affect the lives of current students.

While my reputation as a fundraiser grew, what really made my presidency distinctive were three emphases that dealt with the culture of DePauw. The first emphasis was a plan to diversify the faculty and student body. When I became president of DePauw in the summer of 1986 I enrolled in an American Council of Education workshop for new presidents. Harold Hodginson, a demographer, was the featured speaker. This was my first exposure to the changing demographics of our society. As it turned out this was a pivotal moment in my 22 year presidency. I was captivated by the implications of the growth of blacks and Hispanics and what this might mean for a school like DePauw. I became determined to make DePauw a more inclusive community, and naively believed there would be winners all around if we increased the minority presence at the university. Blacks and Hispanics could benefit from a liberal arts education, and white students would be better equipped to live in the changing world after DePauw.

If Hodginson was the first person to have an impact on my dreams for DePauw, Stuart Watson was the second. Stuart was a marketing genius, the Chairman of Heublein Liquors, and a DePauw trustee. The two of us were walking across the East College lawn in August before my inauguration in October, and Stuart asked me what I hoped to achieve in my presidency. I told him of my tremendous respect for the University, and that I wanted to enhance our reputation outside the Midwest. He replied that this could never happen as long as DePauw was an all-white institution with a Greek system that dominated campus life. Little did we realize then how formative these words would be for the next 22 years.

That fall, in my inaugural address (See Appendix II) I included increasing the diversity of our student body and faculty as one of the three distinctive initiatives of my administration. The other two goals, improving science education and moral reflection, were generally accepted, but the diversity initiative raised more than a few eyebrows. Bob Nelson, my close friend and development consultant, was in the audience when I made the speech and he remarked that I should have seen the expression of surprise on the faces of many of our trustees when I discussed the need to diversify the faculty and student body if DePauw was to be relevant in the 21st Century. It seems I had innocently introduced many alumni to a goal that might change DePauw from the school so many had grown to love and remember.

The first steps were not so difficult. Since we had only one black faculty member, I hired Dorothy Brown, a retired school principal who lived in Greencastle, as a part-time instructor in the Education Department and an advisor to the few black students enrolled at the university. I then hired Delores Gardner as an Assistant Professor in the English Department and Stuart Lord, a recent Princeton graduate, as an assistant chaplain. These three black appointments remained at DePauw for many years and were key to our success.

Additionally, I hired Charles Richardson as the school's first black admissions officer. Under Charles' leadership we concentrated on recruiting blacks from Atlanta, Georgia. We also recruited closer to home, but Atlanta became important to us because DePauw at least had two prominent alumni from there, Vernon Jordan, the civil rights leader, and Bill Allison, a vice president of Coca Cola. We provided transportation from Atlanta to Greencastle for any black students and their parents who were interested in the university. Since we met the full financial need of these students, DePauw became competitive with colleges closer to home. Early on we hosted an admissions weekend for black students and the ballroom of the Union Building was comfortably filled. Bill Allison was the speaker, and as we entered the ballroom, he had tears in his eyes as he told me he never expected to see so many blacks on the DePauw campus. Our efforts were somewhat successful and by 1988 we had 59 black students in the entering class and were on our way.

In the fall of 1988 we faced a significant challenge. October 15 was Old Gold weekend (DePauw's version of Homecoming) and many alumni were back on campus. I spoke to a full house in the Union Building ballroom, where returning alumni had assembled to hear the president talk about the current state of the university. On the walk from the Union Building to Blackstock Stadium to attend the football game Joan Claar, the Dean of Students, mentioned she had heard of a recent disturbance at one of the fraternity parties, but had no details at that point. We continued on to the stadium and settled into our seats to enjoy the game.

At halftime, an incredible event, at least for DePauw, happened. Many of our black students carried signs and posters as they marched peacefully and silently around the track. The consistent message on the signs was "No More Ghetto Parties." Few people knew the significance of this polite demonstration, but the public address announcer invited any interested people to have a conversation with the protesting students, who would be assembled directly under the scoreboard following the game.

After the game concluded I met with several of the students and had a long conversation with Jay Bennett, the President of the African American Student Association. Jay told me about the racist incident that had occurred the night before. He further advised that the students planned a meeting at the African American Students House at 5:00 PM to discuss what response the black students would make. He invited me to attend the meeting, but also made it clear that I did not have to attend as he knew I had other responsibilities that afternoon and evening. (We were hosting a cocktail party and dinner for our significant donors soon after the game.)

I decided to go to the meeting, which I thought would be simply a brief discussion of events the night before. It turns out the theme of the party was "ghetto." White students came dressed as pimps and prostitutes. Some came in blackface and the walls of the fraternity house were covered with posters that praised the Ku Klux Klan, denounced Jesse Jackson, and had words like "spook" written on the wall. Five other fraternities and sororities participated in sponsoring the party. Several black students were invited to the party, and they came with the white students, who did not even think the blacks would be offended. As the discussion proceeded emotions ran high. Many students cried and shared feelings of disbelief. Influenced by Stuart Lord, the students decided to march through campus, pausing at each Greek house that participated in the event. The marchers were to sing "We Shall Overcome" as they proceeded from house to house.

I had to decide whether to march or attend the previously scheduled dinner for our donors. Jay Bennett assured me he would understand if I opted to go to the dinner. I was torn. I wanted to address the donors with a speech I had spent days preparing. But how could I let the march go on without me? My first reaction was to protect the college, as I knew what was about to happen would be widely publicized. I also thought of Walter Harrelson and all the Vanderbilt faculty members who had courageously participated in Civil Rights causes across the South. While their words resonated with me in class, I had never been put in a position where I had to act instead of talk. While college presidents do not normally join student protests I nonetheless decided to march, and by the time it began more than 200 students had assembled. We were joined by Academic Vice President Fred Silander, Jane Funke, the Director of Public Relations, and Joan Claar.

The march was widely covered, both in print and on television. DePauw was in the spotlight, and the aftermath was interesting. Stuart Lord convinced the administration that some further act of closure was needed for the community to heal from racial divisiveness. So on Wednesday following the march on Saturday, a convocation took place in a filled-to-capacity Kresge Auditorium, where each living unit that participated in the party publicly apologized and promised to work for racial harmony. Stuart and I both spoke about our hope for the future, when the campus would be free from racism and become a welcoming community for all. (See Appendix III for the text of my speech.) Yet it did not end there.

The parents of the hosting fraternity members demanded a meeting with me. It was not cordial to say the least! The parents insisted their sons were not the racist people the march portrayed them to be. In fact, they implied that their sons were the real victims, and that I had participated in blaming them by joining the march. They let me know they would not forget this and their hostility remained until their sons graduated. The national office of the fraternity demanded I apologize, which, of course, I did not. Attorneys for the university were concerned about potential lawsuits coming out of the incident and the march. While no lawsuits were ever filed, the lawyers were correct in their assessment of my behavior. The point was that, since the president has the final word in any punishment or appeal of that punishment, by marching I had already prejudiced the process. *My defense was that sometimes one has to act out of a sense of justice no matter the consequences.*

I never really thought of myself as being courageous. I had lived a protected life, one that required little courage. I became involved because of my commitment to diversity. Because I believed that diversity was not only good for DePauw in the educational sense, but that racial justice demanded it, I wanted to see it through, even if it meant some sort of transformation, not only of my own life but that of the university as well.

Now that all my cards were on the table, we went about an even more aggressive recruitment of minority students and faculty. In the admissions process we looked not only at traditional measures like board scores and class rank. We also held personal interviews with all prospective students, looking for measures of social skill and character as predictors of success.

We were significantly helped by our involvement with the Posse Foundation, based in New York City. Under the leadership of Deborah Bial, the Foundation worked primarily with black, Hispanic and Asian students from the inner city, and based on interviews, role playing situations and other communication activities the staff could predict college success. Through the Posse Foundation we were able to recruit more than 20 or so minority students (ten each from New York and Chicago) for each entering class as well as adapt some of their nontraditional predictors of success to minority applicants outside the Posse cities. After only a few years we were able to see 60-70 minority students in each entering class. Perhaps one of the most controversial aspects of our program was that, since we had a cap on enrollment, it was true that some marginal white students were denied admission in deference to minorities. It was not uncommon for the parents of those white students to charge that their sons and daughters were left out because of our strong program to recruit minorities. To some degree they were correct, for we had begun to use race as one of the measures for admission. Against these charges of political correctness we remained steadfast in our belief that diversity was an essential ingredient for a college education.

The recruitment of minority students was but one part of our effort to make DePauw a more diverse community. On a parallel track we were equally determined to recruit minority faculty. With not a single negative vote the faculty passed an ambitious Affirmative Action program. Getting this initiative passed was not difficult. The challenge was the implementation. The administration began to require that all faculty searches include minority candidates, and a member of the administration carefully monitored every search to be certain each department met this requirement. While all faculty had verbally bought into the Affirmative Action program, when the administration began to monitor its progress some faculty charged us with interfering with what had previously been departmental autonomy. They were correct, but this was a necessary step. The previous lack of minorities in the hiring pool was not only evidence of institutional racism, but also evidence of apathy by many faculty, since we were living in a time when if a college posted an opening for a tenure track position most departments would sometimes have over 100 applicants. The trouble was that most of the applicants were white males, and the department made no effort to broaden the pool of candidates.

I mentioned earlier that we were assisted in recruiting minority students because of our success in raising money for scholarships. A similar dynamic was true in recruiting minority faculty. For some time there had been a need to increase the size of the faculty. Enrollment had grown and the teaching load for DePauw's faculty was significantly heavier than the best liberal arts colleges in the Midwest. As we made faculty additions it was less difficult to have inclusive searches, since the department won in two ways. It could become more diverse and increase departmental size at the same time. When I retired 14% of the faculty were minorities, as compared to having only one black faculty member in 1986.

A third emphasis in our diversity effort was to significantly increase the number of black speakers we brought to campus. We hosted well known figures like Spike Lee, the movie director, Charles Barron, a former Black Panther from New York City, and General Colin Powell. We also had educators Manning Marable, bell hooks, Maya Angelo and journalists Carl Rowan and Gwen Ifill as well as civil rights leaders Roger Wilkins, Andrew Young and Jesse Jackson. I well remember Henry Louis Gates, speaking at DePauw during Black History Month, and commenting that he loved Black History Month because he got to meet all his brothers in the airport! To be sure, we celebrated this occasion but we also sought to have a significant minority perspective throughout the school year.

As a result of all this work I learned that being a liberal white person with a few black friends is not enough to change an institution. I never sought to make the white members of the DePauw community feel guilty, although this was sometimes the case. I just wanted all of us to recognize white privilege. Until we had black faculty at DePauw we could not hear firsthand what it was like for them to walk into the local Walmart and be followed through the store, even though they were faculty members at the university. Realizing what it was like to be black and live in Greencastle, we worked to make DePauw a welcoming community. We hosted monthly picnics for the black faculty and worked with the newly established Black Caucus to address any issues that arose. Fortunately for me, through the social events for the black faculty and the workings of the Black Caucus, deep and lasting friendships developed which nurtured a sense of trust between the administration and our new colleagues.

Vice President for Academic Affairs Neal Abraham and I developed our relationships with minority faculty by using somewhat unconventional ways to add blacks to the faculty. For example, when Samuel Autman was a visiting advisor for the student newspaper we found him to be just the kind of person we wanted to attract to the university. Samuel had worked as a newspaper reporter for the *Tulsa World,* the *Salt Lake Tribune,* the *St. Louis Post Dispatch,* and the *San Diego Union Tribune.* Now at DePauw for a semester, his task was to advise the student newspaper and teach one course in journalism. Samuel loved his teaching and the students responded to him with enthusiasm. Neal and I got to know Sam well and we began to discuss with him the possibility of leaving journalism for a faculty position at DePauw. Of course he would need the proper academic credentials, so we used some Presidential Discretionary Funds to enable him to earn an MFA at Columbia University. He then returned to DePauw as a full-time faculty member. Today he is a tenured Associate Professor of English and holds the Richard W. Peck Chair in Creative Writing. He is among the most widely published authors in the entire faculty, and one of the students' most respected professors.

We also supported an outstanding history major by making it possible for her to pursue a PhD. at Loyola University in Chicago. Rhonda Henry then returned to teach at DePauw for several years. However, being a single black woman in Greencastle was a significant challenge, and so Dr. Henry left DePauw for IUPUI, where today she is an Associate Professor of Africana Studies.

My point in mentioning Samuel Autman and Rhonda Henry is that, when desiring to attract black faculty to a campus in a small town in rural Indiana, you have to be opportunistic. You must identify talent and then provide enough financial support for the individuals to obtain the proper academic credentials. This is why we not only supported Mr. Autman and Dr. Henry, but also participated in a program to bring promising black PhD. candidates to DePauw to experience teaching at a small liberal arts college. Through this initiative we were able to hire some outstanding young faculty.

Now that several years have passed and DePauw is indeed a more diverse institution, I realize how indebted we are to those minority students and faculty who came to the university at the beginning of the diversity initiative. To some degree they were always suspect, with some whites feeling minorities were only at DePauw because of the color of their skin. Indeed some black students voiced the belief that we brought them to the university only to educate the white students. They wound up on every committee that had to do with black or brown concerns, and they were often singled out in class to represent the feelings and thoughts of their entire race. But they persevered, and because of the support of many in the community they graduated at a higher rate than the majority white students.

I learned a lot about race relations during my DePauw experience. As a young college president I naively believed that a university, with its allegiance to high ideals, would be a natural place to embrace difference. However, I quickly learned that the university is not a place of racial harmony. It takes a lot of effort to diversify an institution. It is unrealistic to think that black students will easily adapt to the culture of the majority white students. Yet I strongly believed in diversity and I believed in Affirmative Action! Race deserves a special status because so much racism still exists. And your work is not done when you have recruited black students to campus. Many of our students were first generation college students and some struggled financially. We learned from our participation in the Posse Program that you cannot just bring black students into a predominantly white student population and leave them alone. They need mentoring and support.

I talked about diversity for the entire 22 years of my presidency. In the beginning of our program we used consultants like Charles Barron, the former Black Panther, and Debbie Bial of the Posse Foundation to help us understand the needs of the black students we recruited. But we never made this training mandatory, lest it trigger a backlash. We also recruited without having quotas for the admission's office. We simply wanted as many black students as we could recruit. Of course to be successful we had to recruit black faculty, and this was a pipeline issue. We worked on the pipeline by having opportunity hires and using the resources from our financial campaign to make DePauw attractive. *I discovered that if you can raise money you can be successful at almost anything.*

Diversity on college campuses has been a frontline issue for several decades and today some suffer from "diversity fatigue." Diversity efforts can be viewed as political correctness or some colleagues just get tired of hearing about it. But to succeed diversity has to be instilled in everyday life. For 22 years I made the issue of diversity part of my remarks at the opening faculty gathering as well as my welcoming address to the first-year students. (Two of my speeches can be found in Appendix IV.) I was just like the Energizer Bunny: I never stopped. With diversity issues you never arrive. You have to constantly work at it. And you have to carefully describe what you mean by diversity. For me it meant making the DePauw community reflective of the society in which we live. We did not seek minority students to improve the way we looked, but we sought to give minorities the same liberal arts education with internships and international experiences that our white students had enjoyed for decades.

As I look back on the diversity effort at DePauw I have wondered what in my Alabama upbringing prepared me to be a leader in this cause. From my childhood through my early teenage years, I was never concerned about Negroes and racism. I, like everyone else I knew, simply accepted segregation as the way life was. Yet there were several isolated instances that sensitized me to racial injustice. I will mention four.

The first occurred when I was a senior in high school. I had a part-time job selling clothes at Newberry's Department store in downtown Birmingham. I could walk to Newberry's from school, but after work was over I had to ride a Birmingham Transit bus home. The bus had signs separating the "colored" seats from the whites. One morning I remember asking my mother why the blacks had to sit in the back of the bus. Since this was a tense time when the blacks were threatening a bus boycott my mother, not wanting to get into defending segregation, which I am certain she knew was wrong, said simply, "Don't ever ask me that again." While that was the end of our discussion I could sense that my question had struck a nerve and her answer caused me to believe for the first time that there was no good reason for the blacks to sit in the back of the bus.

A second instance of consciousness raising occurred during the Thanksgiving recess at the University of Virginia. My cousin, David Bottoms, was in law school at the university. He had been raised in Auburn, Alabama and when he and his wife along with two other students headed south for Thanksgiving, Dave offered me a ride to Atlanta where I could catch the short flight home to Birmingham. We stopped in Greenville, South Carolina for gas. With a great deal of anger Dave said, "Doesn't that disgust you?" Frankly, at first I did not know what he was talking about but it became clear that he was looking at the signs over the three doors to the public restrooms. One said "Men." Another said "Women," and a third said "Colored." I had seen these signs all my life but had never really thought of life being any other way. Segregation was deeply ingrained in the South and I just accepted it as the way things were. Once Dave called this to my attention I began to see how wrong segregation was...blacks in the back of the bus and blacks using restrooms separate from the whites.

A third instance took place in my sophomore year of college. I was at Birmingham Southern and living at home. We had a black woman, Lilly Mae Hill, who worked for my mother two days a month. She cleaned the house and ironed the clothes. When Lilly finished her work in the early afternoon I would drive her five miles to the black community where she lived. It was customary for blacks to ride in the back seat with the white driver up front. I liked Lilly a lot and I felt uncomfortable with this arrangement. One day I said to Lilly, "You don't have to ride in the back seat. Sit up front with me." She was adamant in denying my invitation explaining that if she rode through her black neighborhood in the front seat of my car other blacks would call her "uppity." Segregation was unchallenged in Sandusky, Alabama in 1963!

The fourth instance had to do with my summer job at Birmingham Rail and Locomotive. Almost all of my coworkers were black. Certainly at work we treated one another as equals and this came easy for me in each of the three summers I worked there. This experience probably contributed to my wanting to treat

Lilly as an equal also. These four instances, while modest in nature, coupled with my seminary education about racial injustice and my experience with the kindergarten at First Methodist Church prepared me in some small ways to be the leader of the diversity program at DePauw.

Under the umbrella of diversity we did more than increase the ethnic diversity of the faculty and student body. We also started a Women's Studies program. In the spring semester of 1987, I approved the hiring of a full-time tenure track position of a Women's Studies Coordinator. This position was made possible by a gift from Janet Prindle, who endowed the program. Janet was a member of the Board of Trustees and a very successful Wall Street banker. While she took some kidding from a few male members of the Board, she proudly stated, "I am for all things that promote women."

Over several years we also made significant changes in the gender makeup of the faculty. In 1986 there were only 32 women faculty in the School of Liberal Arts and the School of Music combined. By 2008, when I retired, that number had risen to 91 or 42% of the faculty.

With the Women's Studies program underway we next turned to the establishment of an Asian Studies program. DePauw had many historic ties to Japan dating back to 1877 when four Japanese students arrived. These four students lay the groundwork for a larger contingent of Japanese students who came to DePauw in later years, and two of these original four students, Sutomi Chinda and Aimaro Soto, became Japanese Ambassadors to the United States. With this historic background I turned to Arthur "Bud" Klauser, the highest ranking American in the Mitsui(USA) Company and a trustee at DePauw to assist in enhancing our ties to Asia. Bud not only shared his financial resources but he contributed his valuable Japanese art collection to the university. In 1990 we were able to attract Paul Watt, a nationally recognized Japanese scholar from Columbia University, to anchor our program. This was quite a feat for a small college located in the cornfields of Indiana. Through Paul's leadership the Asian Studies program grew and in the fall of 2019 we celebrated its 30th anniversary.

If Janet Prindle was the stimulus for the Women's Studies program, Tim Solso was the person most responsible for the expansion of our international program. Tim was a member of the Board of Trustees and the CEO of Cummins Engine Company, headquartered in Columbus, Indiana. When Tim heard me give a speech on the need to recruit more international students, he volunteered to help. Cummins Engine had a substantial presence in both India and China, and Tim opened the door for DePauw. Cummins sponsored a week-long trip for Gwen and me to visit Pune, India. We met with Ravi Pandit, the CEO of

KPIT, a Cummins subsidiary and arranged a program to recruit the children of KPIT employees to come to DePauw. Pandit also implemented an internship program for our students to work at KPIT.

With a robust program to recruit minority students and faculty, the establishment of the Women's Studies program, the beginning of an Asian Studies program, and the enhancement of our international emphasis, the diversity issue had traction at DePauw. Not even the ghetto party, with all its repercussions, had diminished our determination to make DePauw more relevant to the 21st Century.

Even though I began these new initiatives at the University, I did not perceive myself as some sort of trailblazer. In fact, DePauw had many progressive tendencies from its very inception. Founded in 1837, the charter of the institution as approved by the General Assembly of Indiana, stated the university would "forever be conducted on the most liberal principles, accessible to all religious denominations, and designed for the benefit of our citizens in general." It goes on to state DePauw "shall be founded and maintained forever upon a plan most suitable for the benefit of the youth of every class of citizens, and of every religious denomination, who shall be freely admitted to equal advantages and privileges of education, and to all the literary honors of said university, according to their merit, under the direction of the trustees."

In keeping with the liberal spirit of the charter of the university two presidents of the seventeen who preceded me stand out. Matthew Simpson, DePauw's first president, was a gifted speaker, an outspoken supporter of the Union, and a national voice in opposition to slavery. A close friend and advisor to Abraham Lincoln, Simpson spoke at Lincoln's funeral in Springfield, Illinois. DePauw's 13th president, G. Bromley Oxnam, was also a progressive and controversial president. He was an antimilitarist who abolished the entire R.O.T.C. program. He hosted Norman Thomas, the Socialist candidate for president, who opposed the re-election of Herbert Hoover and over 240 students supported Thomas in a straw poll in 1932. In George Manhart's *DePauw Through the Years* the story is told of an Indianapolis alumnus who bitterly opposed Oxnam's views and those of the speakers he brought to campus. Oxnam was accused of indoctrinating students with "sex, socialism, and sovietism." After leaving DePauw in 1936, as a Methodist Bishop, Oxnam was active in national politics and in 1953 he was accused of being a communist. He appeared before the House Un-American Activities Committee on July 21,1953. I mention these two men to point out that the programs I led, while somewhat controversial, were actually modest when compared to the ideals and actions of two of the earlier presidents of the university.

While the ghetto party provided a challenge, two other

incidents also defined the changing DePauw culture. The first dealt with religion and the second with DePauw's Greek system. In 2001 Janis Price was an administrator in the Education Department who supervised student teachers. She made a magazine available to her students from *Focus On the Family* and a student complained that the magazine was anti-gay and hostile to homosexuality. Neal Abraham, the Vice President for Academic Affairs, agreed with the student and concluded it was unprofessional for Janis Price to share such publications with students. I will not attempt to explain all the details of the saga, but instead I will focus on the dynamic, the press coverage that followed and the decisions I had to make.

Dr. Abraham placed Janis Price on probation and reduced her position from full-time to 75% time. She, in turn, sued the university, claiming the university had violated her First Amendment rights and created a hostile environment. The lawsuit gained national attention as Price contended she had been discriminated against because of her religious beliefs. The press on the religious right had a field day. Price was interviewed by Pat Robertson on his television show, "The 700 Club," and DePauw was characterized as a "loser school" that had abandoned its Christian heritage and become pro-homosexual. "The current DePauw administration is anti-Christian," stated Janis Price.

Initially Price won a court verdict based on the jury's belief that DePauw had not followed the procedures in the Academic

Handbook in sanctioning her. DePauw appealed the judgment and eventually saw the issue through the courts until the Indiana Supreme Court overturned the earlier ruling and declared DePauw had not violated Price's religious freedom.

My point in relating this incident is not to retry the court case but to illustrate how vicious the religious right can be in promoting an anti-gay agenda. Of course I had to decide early on whether I supported Vice President Abraham's decision, which I did. While I was not personally involved in the court case, and was never called as a witness, I nonetheless had to articulate DePauw's position for the public. As a result of Abraham's decision Price stated, "DePauw used to have a wonderful reputation, and they still have many wonderful people and programs. But it has changed in the past ten years." Price's view was held by many on the Christian right. One person stated that at DePauw you had to be tolerant of all views but that Christians were not tolerated. An alumnus, Jeffrey Snavely, even wrote a book entitled *Tolerating the Intolerable* which alleged that since I had become president DePauw had promoted a pro-homosexual, anti-Christian agenda.

Because of all the publicity I received hundreds of emails from across the country, mostly from people who had no connection to the university. The emails were among the most hostile that I received during my presidency. Often they were addressed, "Dear Homosexual Loving President..." or some similar words. Many

urged DePauw supporters to stop giving money to the university
as it had become so liberal and politically correct. However, after
all was said and done, DePauw's position was vindicated by the
courts and neither financial support nor student applications were
diminished.

My point in recalling this incident is that sometimes your
value system is tested in the public arena and your values are out
in the open for everyone to see. In both the diversity initiative
and the Janis Price issue, some sought to portray DePauw as
being politically correct and an institution that had betrayed the
Methodist principles on which we were founded. We, on the
other hand, felt we had publicly stood on the principles of non-
discrimination and inclusiveness.

First the ghetto party, then the issue of gays and the Religious
Right and thirdly an issue with DePauw's Greek system…and
all garnered national attention. The Greek issue centered around
the Delta Zeta sorority. For several years the Delta Zeta chapter at
DePauw had struggled with numbers. In a survey by a psychology
professor, students viewed the sorority as "socially awkward,"
perhaps filled with brainy women, many of whom were math and
science majors.

The national headquarters of Delta Zeta was concerned that
the chapter had so few members, and in November of 2006 the
national conducted a membership review and 23 of the 35 women

were given alumnae status (a euphemism for being tossed out).
In December of 2006, shortly before final exams, the headquarters
sent out letters to all 23 women who had been dismissed, stating
they had to move out of the house by the end of January, 2007.
Several of the members who were to be allowed to stay also moved
out in protest of the way their sorority sisters had been treated.
Because of the timing of the review and because of the order to
have so many of the women vacate the house, on December 6
I sent a letter of reprimand to the national office of Delta Zeta.
Student Services worked with the women and assured them the
university would support them and find adequate housing for
them. After exams DePauw had its Winter Term and few students
were on campus. When we reconvened for the second semester
in February I began to interview the women of Delta Zeta—both
those who had left and those who were allowed to stay.

So far the upheaval of the sorority house was a local matter.
The administration was working to support the women and the
faculty circulated a petition in support of the DePauw students
and criticizing the national office. Then, on Sunday, February 10,
the story of Delta Zeta became a national story when Sam Dillon
of *The New York Times* wrote a front page article entitled "Sorority
Evictions Raise Issues of Looks and Bias." The story stated that
of the 23 women who were asked to leave all were overweight or
Korean or Vietnamese. The story was picked up nationally and so

the Delta Zeta saga was publicized from coast to coast.

On February 27, on ABC's "Good Morning America," Robin Roberts interviewed two of the Delta Zetas-one who was asked to leave and one who was invited to stay but refused in protest over the way her sisters had been treated. On national television the students conveyed that those who were asked to leave were terminated because of being overweight or because of their race (black or Asian). In addition to "Good Morning America" the negative attention to DePauw was also picked up by *People Magazine*, CNN, the *Chronicle of Higher Education*, NBC, CBS, MSNBC and *Newsweek*.

While the national attention was a distraction I focused on what was best for the DePauw students. As a result of so much media attention, the Delta Zeta national office posted comments on their website that blamed our students for their dismissal. Supposedly they were not committed enough to the sorority and they were, in fact, responsible for the house's recent struggles. In addition the national office called for a "media freeze" and refused to make any further comments.

In my interviews with students I discovered that none of the sorority members thought race was an issue. Rather it was widely believed that physical appearance was the problem. It became clear to me that the national office's website incorrectly blamed our students and had acted unfairly by asking so many of them to leave the sorority. It was also cruel to inform the students of their status so close to final exams. Furthermore, I concluded that the interviews held with the students were not in depth and that the students were correct in feeling discriminated against.

I called a press conference on March 3, 2007, and because of so much publicity, the room was overflowing with reporters. I announced that as president I felt the way Delta Zeta dealt with our students was incompatible with the way we sought to relate to our students. I further announced that Delta Zeta would not be allowed to open in the fall of 2007, effectively dismissing the sorority from campus. On March 29, *The New York Times* reported that Delta Zeta had filed a lawsuit against DePauw for expelling the sorority from campus. However, in November of 2007 the lawsuit was dropped. We had been successful in our stand against the national headquarters and our students and faculty supported our position that no Greek organization would be allowed to base their membership on stereotypes.

While we raised a significant amount of money, built many buildings, enlarged the size of the faculty and made DePauw a more diverse institution, the ghetto party incident, the Janis Price lawsuit and the conflict with the Delta Zeta national remain three of my most vivid memories of being President of DePauw. While each of these instances were challenging, they were, in some sense, liberating because I was forced to take public stands against racism, homophobia and the superficiality of the Greek system.

I have discussed some of the successes I had at DePauw, but I also made mistakes. I will mention three. In my haste to hire black faculty and staff I did make some errors. I sometimes placed blacks in high administrative posts who had little or no training for their jobs. On the whole they were good people, but I was wrong to believe that with the proper support they could grow into their responsibilities. While I see no value in naming the people I am referring to, I will make one notable exception.

In January of 1987, I received a telephone call from Dick Tinkham, a Depauw alumnus who lived in Indianapolis. Dick told me how much he supported our diversity effort, and then spoke of his relationship with Wilma Rudolph, who lived in Indianapolis at the time. He then asked if I would be interested in hiring Ms. Rudolph as our women's track coach. I was blown away by this possibility. Wilma Rudolph was a nationally known Olympic Champion, having won three gold medals in 1960, a feat that caused the Associated Press to name her "Woman Athlete of the Year."

I interviewed Ms. Rudolph, and she talked about the possibility of summer clinics at DePauw to train future runners and hosting a national workshop for the top American track coaches. What I did not foresee was that Wilma Rudolph was more interested in her compensation than in working with the women's track team on a daily basis. She was sporadic in her attendance at track practice, and when she did show up, she had a striking presence. She frequently dressed in a full length black fur coat, an unusual sight for the track at Blackstock Stadium. Wilma Rudolph lasted less than one year at DePauw before I had to release her. I had been too quick to assume that because she talked a persuasive game, she would follow through.

You may have surmised from our significant fundraising success that I could be seduced into thinking all was well with DePauw. In fact, when the Campaign for DePauw was finished in 2000, the trustees and I planned a Gala in Indianapolis to celebrate our accomplishment. Our major donors and all the faculty and staff were invited. Then, on Tuesday, April 25, before the Gala was to be held on Friday, the 28th, I had a visit from John Dittmer, a member of DePauw's history department. John brought me a copy of a letter he had written entitled, "Why I Won't Be at the Gala." His reasoning was that for years the university had failed to pay a living wage to our hourly workers, food service employees, buildings and grounds personnel and departmental secretaries. Our defense was that while we admitted our salaries were low, they were competitive with the local market. John pointed out that, while this might be correct, our comparison group was in Putnam County, one of the poorest counties in Indiana. He said he would not distribute the letter if I would do something to raise the wages of our hourly staff. I thanked John for coming to me before he published the letter, but I also told him there was nothing I could do in the immediate future as the budget for 1999-2000 had already been set.

John circulated the letter around campus and it received a lot of positive support from the faculty and staff. That May, at commencement, the student speaker even referenced the low wages of DePauw's hourly employees. I reluctantly agreed that both John and the student were correct, and so, in the fall we raised the wages in question.

The third issue I may have been mistaken about is the so-called "open file" policy that I instituted in the year I was Acting President. At the time I believed I acted out of necessity to address the faculty's suspicion of the administration. In my 22 years as President I made all of my tenure and promotion decisions based on what was in a faculty member's personnel file. I was challenged only once with a grievance, and the Faculty Appeals Panel upheld my decision.

However, in looking back, the "open file" policy had some unintended consequences. Although we sought to support faculty development projects with sufficient stipends, too few faculty members participated. With no research component for tenure and promotion and no outside evaluations, as had been the case with my predecessor, very few faculty were denied tenure or promotion. Over time this, of course, meant DePauw had a very high percentage of tenured faculty. This was not a problem for my administration because student enrollment was stable. (Actually, we operated most years at capacity.) However when my successors saw enrollment numbers decline, such a highly-tenured faculty became problematic.

I have attempted to deal honestly with my mistakes as well as the challenges I faced with decisions that garnered national attention. Of course, there were many other decisions that mattered deeply to the DePauw community which were not widely publicized. I will mention five.

In the first year of my presidency Tim Ubben, a DePauw trustee, came into my office with an unusual proposal. He said, "I am going to give you a lot of money, but you will not like it." I thought this was an unusual way to start a conversation, so I asked him to explain. Tim thought prospective students might be put off by coming to college in a small town where presumably nothing important ever happened. It was his intention to endow the Tim and Sharon Ubben Lecture Series, which would bring thought leaders from throughout the world to DePauw. Tim knew this would be expensive, so he took it upon himself to cover all the speakers' fees so the university could not be criticized for spending large amounts of money for visiting speakers. This had, in fact, caused a great deal of trouble at other colleges when large fees paid to speakers had become public.

As a result of Mr. and Mrs. Ubben's generosity, the university was able to attract leaders from all over the world. Gwen and I had the privilege of hosting them in our home and introducing them to our students and faculty. We had leaders of state Margaret Thatcher, John Major, Tony Blair, Benazir Bhutto, Shimon Peres, Mikhail Gorbachev, and Willie Brandt. We hosted US leaders like Colin Powell, Zbigniew Brzezinski, Paul Bremer and Barbara Bush. We were also able to have as our guests commentators on humanitarian crises like Elie Wiesel, Jesse Jackson, Harry Belafonte, Spike Lee, Julian Bond, Roger Wilkins and Doris Kearns Goodwin. Since DePauw had a strong journalistic tradition we hosted David Broder, Ken Burns, George Will, Bob Woodward, Gwen Ifill, Gloria Borger and David Gergen. I could go on and on about how the lecture series enriched our campus.(A complete list of Ubben Lecturers is listed in Appendix V.) Suffice it to say it was an honor to meet such dignitaries and converse with true thought leaders. Few college presidents have this opportunity, and it came about as a result of a gift Tim Ubben said would make me angry.

Second, when I became president of DePauw in 1986, 90% of the student body was affiliated with the Greek system. For decades new member recruitment(rush) took place the week before school started in the fall. The students would arrive a week early and the women would move into a dormitory where they would live for their first year in college. The men, on the other hand, would live in the dorms for only the week during rush and then, if invited to join a fraternity, would move directly into the fraternity house.

I found this to be problematic for several reasons. First, as we recruited high school students for our first-year class we could tell the women where they would live once on campus. We would then have to tell the men that where they lived would be dependent on the result of new member recruitment for the fraternities, an anxiety-producing situation. Second, it seemed an antiquated practice to treat the men and women differently. Did we think the women were in need of the support and supervision of the resident hall counselors while the men were mature enough to live on their own in the fraternities? Experience seemed to indicate that 18-year-old men did indeed need the supervision and support of the residence hall staff.

To correct this situation was a problem. For generations the university had depended on the Greek system to house a majority of our students. As a result, if we mandated that men should live in a residence hall for their first year, we were not capable of providing enough housing. The only solution was to build a new dormitory and, upon my recommendation, the Board of Trustees voted to do just that. This proved to be unpopular with many of the alumni. Not only was the university abandoning a long tradition, but moving the first-year men out of the fraternity houses and into a residence hall effectively caused the fraternities to lose the rent the first-year men paid to their individual houses. Moving ahead with the plan to build the dorm caused many alumni to charge that the new president was anti-Greek. Nonetheless, we did build the new residence hall and it was dedicated in 1989. It was named Humbert Hall after the former beloved president of DePauw, Russell Humbert.

The advantages for the university were several. Now that all first-year students were living in university housing, new member recruitment could come later in the year, after students had settled into the academic program. Also, for the first time in decades, we could treat the women and men the same. As I look back, it was undoubtedly the right thing to do, but the charge that I was anti-Greek plagued my presidency.

A third controversial decision concerned the School of Nursing. The School had begun in the early 1950's, and 35 years later over 700 nurses had graduated. That this was a high quality program could not be questioned. However, there were two systemic problems with the nursing school. Students in the school spent their first two years on the DePauw campus taking the required science courses and their liberal arts electives. The students then moved to the Methodist Hospital in Indianapolis for their last two years. This split campus was unappealing to many prospective students. A second issue was that the DePauw tuition was much higher than the Indiana University School of Nursing, and so if you wanted to become a nurse the cost to attend DePauw was a significant obstacle.

Because of these challenges enrollment in the School of Nursing was low and the deficits of the school were increasing. However, because of the high quality of the program, in 1987 we decided to put more resources into the School of Nursing. We hired an admissions counselor dedicated to the nursing school and stipulated that the school had three years to be able to recruit a minimum of 25 students in a first-year class. Even with the three year grace period and the support in the admissions effort, the enrollment fell short of the established goal. On October 26, 1990 the Board of Trustees, upon my recommendation, voted to close the nursing school. We were to phase out the program for the 50 students already in the school and at the end of the 1993-94 school year the school was to close. Because of the program's high quality, this was a difficult decision, but it was clear to me that the School of Nursing could never be self-sufficient.

A fourth interesting decision that I made would be seldom noticed, but I believe it was significant in the college's history. Since DePauw was a Methodist institution, it was customary for nine members of the Board of Trustees to be elected by the annual conferences of the church. As a result of this system, several Methodist clergy found themselves elected trustees. While I had no objection to clergy serving on the board, it was my observation that they had less loyalty and enthusiasm for the university than did the alumni on the board. I proposed to Bishop Leroy Hodapp that, since the clergy were most interested in engaging with the religious life on campus, we establish a United Methodist Council composed of clergy and lay persons from both annual conferences. The Council would meet semi-annually and receive information about the religious life on campus. The Council then became the avenue for the church to have a relationship with the university.

As for the Board of Trustees, the Methodist Bishop of Indiana would retain a place on the Board, but the rest of the Board would be elected by the Board itself. Thus the Board became a self-perpetuating entity and our charter was changed on April 23, 1993 to reflect this. This action was important for two reasons: it allowed us to fill the Board with persons who had tremendous loyalty to DePauw, and it allowed the university to escape any attempt by conservatives to elect a slate of trustees who were theologically opposed to social issues like gay marriage and the offering of insurance to same sex couples. This was a dynamic that played out at some other Methodist colleges and universities but fortunately DePauw was spared this drama.

A fifth significant event occurred on Sunday morning, April 7, 2002. Gwen and I were in church when we heard one loud siren after another. No one inside the church knew what was going on, but it was clear that something bad had happened. When church was over, the sirens kept blaring and I realized fire trucks had been called to DePauw. I drove the few blocks to campus only to see that Rector Hall, one of our primary residence halls, was on fire. Flames were shooting from the roof and numerous fire trucks were on the scene to fight the blaze. I found Bill Nugent, the local fire chief, in the crowd and asked him to assess the situation. He replied that the building would probably be lost. That was the bad news. But the good news was that he thought all of our students were safely out of the flaming structure. What a relief! Sunday morning, with so many students in bed asleep, was a terrible time for a fire.

The firefighters were courageous and extremely competent. By noon the blaze was under control. Unfortunately, the building was severely damaged and we had 150 students with nowhere to live. The students' clothes, computers, musical instruments and all other belongings were either lost or damaged. The campus community quickly organized to address the situation. We set up headquarters in the Student Union Building. Phones were made available for students to call their parents and let them know they were safe. Food was prepared, and the community began to bring clothes for the students who had lost everything. Sororities, fraternities and dormitory staff mobilized to provide new housing for those affected. We were relieved that no one was injured.

In the next week we were able to assess the damage, and it

was determined that Rector Hall could indeed be repaired, as the four exterior walls were intact even though the interior of the building was badly damaged. The repairs might take as long as two years to complete and we had to find a way to replace the 150 beds we had lost before the incoming class would arrive at the end of the summer. We had to act quickly. We employed the CSO architectural firm in Indianapolis to design some sort of housing that could be constructed in four months. They were able to design numerous duplexes and small apartments that could meet our deadline. The problem was where to build them, as the campus was short on space.

The solution was to buy up residential properties close to the campus, which we did. We purchased numerous old houses, tore them down and built the new duplexes and apartments. On the surface, this seemed like the perfect solution, but the decision became controversial. Since the university was tax exempt, every house we purchased came off the tax rolls of the city. Many people in town were upset by this, since Greencastle was always financially challenged and here was this seemingly wealthy university contributing to the city's financial woes. This dynamic, coupled with the congestion surrounding the construction of the new living units, made us unpopular with many of the city's residents.

Fortunately for the university, we were able to have all the construction finished by the end of the summer, and so we had housing for all our students. Building the apartments for student housing proved to be so popular with students that we decided not to rebuild Rector Hall. Instead we constructed Rector Village, a group of seven buildings with apartment-style units. Thus, what had begun as a tragedy ended up as an opportunity to offer flexibility for student housing.

In 2007, I had completed 21 years as president of DePauw and I announced that I would retire in 2008. I was only 64 years old, but many of the trustees were beginning to talk about another financial campaign and a few even mentioned a goal of $500 million. Such an effort might have lasted at least five years and I did not see myself being president at age 69, so 2008 was a good time to step down.

I did not cut my ties with DePauw, and instead became the first Director of the Janet Prindle Institute for Ethics. The Institute had enjoyed an unusual beginning. Since DePauw had a tradition of producing so many CEOs as well as outstanding journalists and community leaders, we were seriously considering starting a leadership institute. To help us think about this, we invited a team from the Kravis Leadership Institute at Claremont McKenna College in California to attend the spring, 2005 Board of Visitors meeting. Their purpose was to describe their program and let us explore how we might start a similar emphasis at DePauw.

We also invited David Smith, a philosopher from the Poynter Center at Indiana University, to speak about the role of ethics in leadership. David was so eloquent that we decided we wanted not a leadership institute but an ethics institute. With the help of David Smith and John Roth, a visiting professor of philosophy from Claremont McKenna, we began to put our ideas on paper. We wanted our students to leave the university with a discontent about the injustices of the world, and we wanted to assist them in developing values that were more than private taste.

But how might we fund such an endeavor? We turned to Janet Prindle. A Wall Street banker with Neuberger Berman, Janet invested only in companies that did not engage in discriminatory practices, did not sell tobacco, weapons or nuclear power, and were environmentally friendly. Janet immediately warmed to the idea of an ethics institute for DePauw and she committed $10 million for a building to house the institute and bear her name. In 2008 the Prindle Institute was in its new building in our Nature Park and it was the first building in Indiana to be Gold-Rated and certified by the U.S. Green Building Council as a LEED building.

As the first director of the institute I wanted to develop an ethics program for faculty and students. In a way I was returning to my first love, as I had been the chaplain at Birmingham Southern and the Assistant Dean of Vanderbilt Divinity School. I wanted to help students think about right and wrong and explore their beliefs and values. Such a task was too great for one person to tackle alone, and in the early days of the Institute I was assisted by Martha Rainbolt of the English Department and Bob Steele from the Pulliam Center for Contemporary Media.

As I look back over the many years of my presidency, I realize how controversial it was at times. While controversy can take a toll on any president, I always had the unwavering support of my wife, Gwen. When my critics were the most vocal, she calmly encouraged me to do what I felt was in the best interest of the university. She was a terrific First Lady! Gwen made everyone feel welcome at DePauw.

While nothing in her background prepared her to host the world leaders brought to the university by the Ubben Lectures, she did so with a graciousness the DePauw community appreciated. She attended performances by the School of Music, the theatrical performances of the Drama Department, the many athletic events and alumni gatherings across the country. When I made the many speeches a college president is called upon to make, she was a positive critic and the one person I most wanted to please. And she did her best to keep me humble.

While I may have been tempted to be seduced by the trappings of the office, Gwen would often remind me, "Remember, this is not about you." Yet with all this DePauw activity, she did manage to cultivate some of her own interests. She was a docent at the

Indianapolis Museum of Art, took harp lessons from Harriet Moore in the School of Music and earned a Library of Science Degree from Indiana University which allowed her to serve as the Librarian of DePauw's Art Department.

During my presidency I had the opportunity to serve on several nonprofit boards including the Joyce Foundation in Chicago, the Posse Foundation in New York City and the Center for Leadership Development in Indianapolis. A fourth board was the most unusual one for me. It was the Board of Trustees of Seabury Western Theological Seminary in Evanston, Illinois and it opened another interesting chapter in my life. In 2009 I was serving as the chair of the board when the president left for another position, and I was asked to become the interim President and Dean. So I left the Prindle Institute and took on a new challenge which combined my desire to do good things with my ego to want to lead. One child observed, "Dad always likes to be president of things." Perhaps she was correct but I never fancied myself being the president of a seminary. Given my exit from the ministry and my liberal theology, it was an unusual turn of events. Even Gwen said, "I cannot believe you are the president of a seminary. Did they not even ask what you believed?" To be sure, I was never questioned by the Seabury trustees to determine whether I was theologically suited to lead the school. Rather my appointment was a practical one. I was the only trustee who had some experience in higher education and who had the time to serve.

Like many Episcopal seminaries, Seabury had serious financial problems and had, in effect, declared financial exigency. We were left with only a few students and fewer faculty, but the seminary owned some desirable property. We negotiated the sale of our property to Northwestern University, paid off our debt and set about to use the remaining assets to develop a new vision of theological education with $25 million in endowment. We joined with Bexley Hall Seminary in Columbus, Ohio to form a federation of two seminaries and rented space in the Lutheran Center in Chicago. I divided my time between Chicago, Columbus and our new home in Athens, GA.

I retired from Seabury in 2012 and began consulting for the Episcopal Church. Bill Sachs, an Episcopal priest in Richmond, Virginia and I worked as a team, holding leadership seminars for priests and laity with several parishes, the Consortium for Endowed Episcopal Parishes and the College of Bishops of the Episcopal Church. I had known Bill from our graduate school days at Vanderbilt Divinity School and our work together at Seabury Western. We based a lot of our work about leadership on our own experiences and out of a joint effort we had participated in between Seabury and the Kellogg Business School at Northwestern University. The basic idea was to take many of the insights about leadership and marketing from the business school and apply them to the church. Like business leaders, priests face challenges running their organizations. They sometimes oversee a large staff and expensive physical plants. Seminaries may do a wonderful job in theological training, but not so much on the management side. We hoped to address this shortcoming.

One of the most interesting assignments was with the College for Bishops and it continued for three years. During this time, Bill and I proposed a leadership program which we hoped would be sponsored by the College and made available not only to bishops but to parish priests and lay people who were interested in applying learnings from other nonprofit organizations. We planned to deliver our curriculum through both conferences and an interactive website. While the College was initially encouraging, the idea was ultimately turned down, I suspect because many of the bishops maintained that the church was so distinctive an organization that no business principles could apply.

Undaunted by this rejection, we then initiated conversations between the Virginia Theological Seminary and the Darden School of Management at the University of Virginia. We developed a week-long curriculum on leadership and it seemed to be appreciated by both the seminary and Darden. The problem was that the participation of the Darden faculty was expensive. Such a week would cost over $200,000 and no one believed the clergy could afford paying a tuition that would offset the cost. We then sought outside funding from lay people. Despite the enthusiasm from a handful of people, we were unable to secure adequate resources and the project, though full of promise, was unable to go forward. By the time of this rejection I was 74 years old and I had finished all my consulting work with the Episcopal Church.

With this I believed my work with the Episcopal Church was finished. Then the unexpected happened again. In December of 2018 Gary Hall, the retired Dean of the National Cathedral and former President and Dean of Seabury Western Seminary, called to invite me to become a member of the Board of Trustees of the Episcopal Divinity School at Union Seminary in New York. The invitation was seconded by Bishop John Rabb, the retired Suffragan Bishop of the Diocese of Maryland and an old friend from DePauw. I was flattered to be asked to do anything at my age, and so I accepted. What an honor to attend my first meeting and be in a building where Paul Tillich, Dietrich Bonhoeffer and Wilhelm Pauck had taught! Perhaps a fitting end to my career. Serving on this Board and writing these memoirs remain my last professional projects...unless, of course,the unexpected happens again.

≈

CHAPTER THREE
HOW DO WE MAKE DECISIONS?

IN THE FALL OF 2010, BOB STEELE INVITED ME TO GIVE THE KEYNOTE LECTURE AT THE JANICE PRINDLE INSTITUTE FOR ETHICS UNDERGRADUATE HONORS CONFERENCE. The topic he asked me to address was how we make decisions. Bob and I enjoyed a close relationship. I had recruited him from the Poynter Institute for Media Studies in St. Petersburg, Florida to come to DePauw as the Pulliam Professor of Journalism, and we taught a course on leadership together. Then, when I retired, Bob became the second Director of the Prindle Institute. Addressing the topic seemed like a natural thing to do. Having been the President of DePauw for over two decades, I made many decisions affecting the lives of others. I tried to approach my analyses with a moral compass, but I had never dissected the process. Such a task proved to be more complicated than I imagined.

In preparing my presentation I read a great deal. So much, in fact, that I was reminded of a line in P. F. Kluge's book, *Alma Mater*. When he listened to President Phillip Jordan's opening convocation address at Kenyon College, Kluge remarked, "He (Jordan) quoted a lot of other people," implying that Jordan had few ideas of his own. As I developed my lecture I did have many ideas of my own, but I was also influenced by the writing of theologians Karen Armstrong and Parker Palmer, moral philosopher Susan Neiman, psychologist Jonathan Haidt, political philosopher Michael Sandel, Chip Heath of the Stanford Business School, and Joseph Bodaracco of the Harvard Business School.

With these influences, coupled with my own reflections about decisions I had made, I developed the following model. In explaining it I could never do justice to all the research on decision making, so I have dispensed with the scholarly apparatus, such as including numerous footnotes, and chosen instead to simply list books that influenced me in a bibliography.

There is much debate about how we make decisions. We are influenced by numerous voices – I call them "annoying voices" because they are often in conflict with one another. We use reason, deal with our emotions, listen to the advice of others and attempt to apply our basic values in making decisions. All of these voices came into play when I wrestled with my responses to the ghetto party, the conflict with the Religious Right over homosexuality, the move to build a dormitory and house the first-year men, the Rector residence hall fire, and the closing of the School of Nursing.

So, out of my experience, how do we make decisions given the many voices that compete to influence us? Many of us believe we primarily use reason. This has been the case since the early Greek philosophers. When confronted with a decision we use our minds. We try to figure things out. We look at all the options, and apply our experiences. We recall our stories and use what we have learned in school. It is this ability to reason that makes us human. We think about the future, and we imagine how things might be. We ask if our potential decision makes sense. Can we prove it? We like to get at the facts.

But relying on reason alone to make a decision presents a problem. We not only have a head, we also have a heart. And sometimes facts just do not matter to the heart. Seemingly reasonable people can act irrationally. For example, I am a member of the Board of Directors of the Joyce Foundation, and we work on preventing gun violence. Gun ownership advocates are emotionally invested in their cause, and they believe owning a gun makes one more safe. Actually, research indicates just the opposite, but to the emotional gun lobby, the facts just do not seem to matter.

Since ancient Greece we have believed humans are rational animals. However, large bodies of material, developed by neuroscientists, argue that for generations we have misunderstood how decisions are made. Some neuroscientists believe we are not designed to be rational. We actually make choices emotionally, and then we look for facts to support them. Science has revealed the importance of emotion in making decisions and, without going into all the details, most of us can agree that our inner voice does impact how we behave. We want to know if we can live with the consequences. This is what Joseph Bodaracco calls "sleep test ethics." After we make an important decision, we want to rest easy at night. To be sure, we use our minds, but we want to feel good about our actions. We want to feel we have done the right thing. We want to follow our hearts. Yet before we adopt the position that sleep ethics are normative, we have to admit that we know of some people who can act badly and still sleep soundly. Also, many of us have had the experience of knowing we have done the right thing and we still lie awake at night. This was true of me after the ghetto party and the other incidents I have described.

Sometimes when we face an important decision, we just instinctively know what is right and we feel this way without using our rational faculties. Jonathan Haidt describes an experience while teaching an undergraduate seminar. He told his students a story about Julie and Mark, two siblings on a vacation in Paris. Julie and Mark had always been close, and one night after a delicious dinner and a bottle of wine, they decided to have sex. Even though Julie practiced birth control, Mark used a condom. The next morning they discussed their experience, and both felt they had been drawn closer together. Nonetheless they decided never to do it again. Had this experience been wrong, the students were asked? "Yes," they all answered. And "Why?," asked Haidt. "Because incest can cause birth defects," said one student. But Haidt reminded them both Julie and Mark had used birth control. Another student responded that incest would ruin their relationship and Haidt reminded them that both siblings said they felt closer the morning after. No matter what the emotional objection, Haidt reminded the students of the facts until one student responded, "We just know it was wrong!" Indeed, we just know some things are wrong. Intuition can sometimes guide our actions.

While it may be true that emotion can lead to a good outcome, as in the case of Mark and Julie, making decisions based on emotion or intuition can become as problematic as using reason alone. I say this because sometimes our emotions are in conflict with one another. When I was the Assistant Dean of the Divinity School at Vanderbilt, we hosted a breakfast for several business executives in the Nashville community. Thomas Ogletree, a Professor of Ethics, was the speaker. In the question and answer period following Tom's presentation Maxie Jarman, the Chief Executive of Jarman Shoes, asked a question. Jarman stated his company had a shoe factory in South America. The company paid good wages and employed many people who had previously been jobless. The problem he faced was that the government was now demanding a bribe to allow the shoe plant to continue to operate. What should he do? Instinctively, he was opposed to paying bribes. But if he refused to pay, many employees would be out of work, destined to return to poverty. This happened more than 40 years ago, and I cannot recall exactly how Ogletree answered. I only remember how perplexed he was. A true dilemma for the professor, sorting out the competing values of two goods – two admirable values in opposition to one another. Not wanting to pay a bribe and not wanting to contribute to joblessness.

Another instance of values being in conflict with one another is more personal. When my father was in the hospital being treated for lung cancer, he had come to the realization that he would soon die. One day, when we were alone, he asked me, the newly-ordained Methodist minister, what heaven would be like. Having graduated from the liberal seminary at Emory University and exposed to the many myths of my childhood faith, I was speechless. What could I say? Should I lie and repeat what we were taught as children, that he would be in a state of bliss, reunited with those loved ones who had preceded him in death? Or should I be honest and just say that, despite three years of seminary training, I had no idea what the afterlife was about, or even if there was one. I chose to simply say that I did not know, and my father became angry at my inability to answer his question. Looking back, I was torn between two very different and positive feelings. I wanted to be compassionate because I loved my father, but at the same time I wanted to be intellectually honest. Both values I cherished were in conflict with one another.

Even with the problem of conflicting emotions there is still much contemporary thinking that promotes trusting our intuition. Steve Jobs, the founder of Apple, observed that we should not let the voices of others drown out our inner voice. We need to have the courage to follow our hearts. Somehow our intuition can know what we truly want to become. However, even if we believe Jobs that decisions are based on instinct, we still have to explain them. We cannot simply say, "It just feels right." Our decision may entail an argument between what we think and what we feel, and this makes certainty difficult. But I do not want to dismiss Sleep Test Ethics entirely. Our intuition can play a valuable role. The issue is how to use the sleep test, how to regulate our emotions, and we do this by thinking, by processing them.

There can be a third factor in making decisions. We do not have to be alone. We can recruit advisors. Moral reflection need not be a solitary pursuit. Michael Sandel of Harvard University argues we need an interlocutor, a fellow citizen, a friend, a neighbor to assist us, and this is a long tradition going back to Socrates. In thinking of my experiences as president of DePauw I am certain that my presidency was enhanced by the caliber of the people in my cabinet. I had three women, three blacks, two people with college age children and four older white men. Individually we had our shortcomings, but collectively we made wise decisions. Our diversity allowed us to overcome what is now called "confirmation bias," the tendency to just listen to the facts that support what we already believe. This phenomenon has also been discussed by Doris Kearns Goodwin in her book *Team of Rivals,* where she discusses Lincoln's ability to promote and tolerate different views as one of the keys to his leadership.

In getting beyond the echo chamber of confirmation bias, Chip Heath of Stanford University tells the story of Alfred P. Sloan, the former head of General Motors. Sloan had convened his advisors to address an important problem. Everyone, without dissent, agreed on the path to be followed. Sloan, in his wisdom, adjourned the meeting and said they would come back together when someone could make a counter argument, his way of breaking out of the echo chamber.

As we make decisions we use our intellect, become emotionally influenced, and listen to the opinions of others. These other voices can be not only interlocutors but also mentors, and mentors must not simply be people who make us feel good. The best mentors are those who provide a kind of "tough love." Bob Nelson served this role for me. I have already described the success we had in fundraising, and this was in no small part a result of Bob's counsel. But this was not always smooth. I can recall many times when heated arguments preceded the formalization of our plans. There was no echo chamber in our discussions, and this was of significant benefit to the university.

A second advisor who broadened my horizons was Sally Davis, a young black woman I hired as Assistant to the President. She always spoke the truth to me about race even if it made me uncomfortable. Sally and I had a very interesting experience in Washington D.C. Carl Rowan, a prominent journalist and political

activist and the founder of Project Excellence, had invited me to
be the keynote speaker at an admissions event for prospective
students at the headquarters of the Gannett organization.
Assembled there were over 500 black students and their parents.
To be in attendance, the students had to have at least a B average in
high school and be recommended by their high school counselor.
My job was to encourage them to apply to college. Sally and I
walked in the room together, and I remarked to her that I was the
only white person in the room. "No," she said, "All the waiters
are white." I had not noticed. *We sometimes need the eyes of others to
correct what we overlook ourselves.*

Our brains, our emotions and the influence of other people all
impact our decisions. But is that all there is to decision making? Is
there a role for personal values in the process? Put another way,
is there a place for idealism? Is there not some value in thinking
about how the world ought to be? Whether it be the dynamic
of responding to the ghetto party, challenging the Religious
Right, confronting the national office of a sorority or building a
dormitory to house the first-year men, my values of compassion
and inclusion were always paramount. While the truth may tell
us how the world is, morality tells us how the world ought to be,
and our ideals should have force and consequences. Values must
inform our decisions, and our morality becomes a series of choices
about how we treat people. The Golden Rule is an excellent value

to follow, but it will challenge us. The Golden Rule is actually a radical idea when we consider the welfare of others as important as our own. It implies that we are all equal and that no one is privileged over the other.

The Golden Rule may lead us to believe that moral decisions are influenced by sympathy. We want to treat others fairly because we all know what it means to be treated unfairly. Some neuroscientists have argued this concept of sympathy is hardwired into our brains. For example, if presented with statistics on world hunger we might give a small amount of money to help. But, instead of statistics, if we are shown the faces of hungry children, we are inclined to be much more generous. Mother Theresa has been quoted as saying if she only looked at the masses she would never act. But if she looked into the eyes of one, she would.

This desire to be empathetic, to treat others as we would like to be treated is captured well in the following Buddhist poem from the Sutta Nipata which Karen Armstrong introduced to me.

Let all things be happy! Weak or strong, of high, middle, or low estate, small or great, visible or invisible, near or far away, alive or still to be born-May they all be perfectly happy!

Let nobody lie to anybody or despise any single being anywhere.

May nobody wish harm to any single creature out of anger or hatred!

Let us cherish all creatures, as a mother her only child!

May our loving thoughts fill the whole world, above, below, across-

without limit: our love will know no obstacles-a boundless goodwill toward the whole world, unrestricted, free of hatred or enmity.

Whether we are standing or walking, sitting or lying down, as long as we are awake we should cultivate this love in our heart. This is the noblest way of living.

I have described how the intellect, emotions, the influence of others and one's values potentially come into play when important decisions have to be made. I do not mean for this description to be too theoretical, for in my experience, there are also some practical guides. In approaching decisions it is important to see the grayness of life, to see all sides of an issue. You need to step outside of your own belief system and realize most significant decisions have multiple publics. As president of the university you quickly realize the students, faculty and alumni seldom want the same thing, and it is impossible to meet the expectations of all of them. This underscores the need to be loyal to core beliefs or indeed you will seldom ever sleep well at night.

Second, given the complexity of many different publics and the interplay between the intellect, emotions and value systems, it is best to exhibit genuine humility. You must not get caught up in the trappings of position or authority. This came home to me early in my presidency. In October of 1986 I was to be inaugurated the eighteenth president of DePauw and this was obviously an important day for me. Gwen and I decided to take the children out of school for the event, and it fell to me to collect our daughter, Leslie. On the way from school to the university she observed that I was nervous, and she asked why. I explained to her that aside from Gwen's and my wedding day and her birth and the birth of her brother, this was probably the most important day of my life. Then, from the mouth of a twelve-year-old, came words that I still remember. "Dad, it's not that big a deal." A humbling experience indeed, but a lesson to remember. During my presidency I hope I had the genuine humility to make good decisions.

A third lesson I learned is the value of solitude. We live in a world of instant communication, and we are smothered with information. It is a challenge to reflect on the value of what we do. With so many publics wanting to influence our decisions, it is important to concentrate on one's core values. Solitude is the act of being alone with ourselves, allowing us to be more concerned with what is going on within us, rather than what is going on around us. Sometimes, when those who oppose our decisions are so noisy, the best path is to be silent. When Janis Price sued the university, my critics charged that I was pro-homosexual and unChristian. One person even took out an ad in the local paper that was critical of my leadership and urged people to quit giving money to the university. I was angry, and my first reaction was to strike back. Upon further reflection though, I chose to keep silent, and I discovered that sometimes silence can be beautiful.

Embracing solitude requires good time management skill, not in the technical sense, but in making time to assess how your basic values should influence decisions, and what you must do to remain true to who you are. You must not confuse activity with productivity. You cannot do everything, and you cannot respond to every criticism, but you must choose those paths where you can really make a difference.

I have described several annoying voices that may interact as we make decisions. Reason, emotion, the opinions of others and our core values may seem to compete with one another, and this in the midst of demanding schedules filled with distractions.

And yet there is one other important voice I have yet to mention: the desire for certainty. We naturally want to be certain we are doing the right thing, but we can never let the longing for certainty handcuff us when there is a need to make a decision. We will entertain competing hypotheses, and we will remind ourselves continuously that we may, in fact, not know what might result from our actions. But we have to decide! It takes courage to live in this dynamic, to constantly interrogate ourselves, even as we acknowledge we live under the cloud of uncertainty. This uncertainty cannot impede us, but reminds us of how humble we must be. Unknowing is an essential part of the human condition. I am reminded of the famous quote of the philosopher, Bertrand Russell, "The fundamental cause of the trouble is that in the modern world the stupid are cocksure while the intelligent are full of doubt."

If we do not have clarity of values, our critics will prevail. Living into our values means we do more than talk about them. We apply them in practice. In doing so, we may make others uncomfortable, but we realize we cannot be appreciated by everyone. After we have applied reason, wrestled with our emotions, and listened to the counsel of others, being true to our core values is the only way we can survive and thrive.

❧

CHAPTER FOUR

THE ROLE OF RELIGION IN MY LIFE

I HAVE SHARED THE STORY OF MY UPBRINGING AND MY CAREER, AS WELL AS SEVERAL ILLUSTRATIONS ABOUT DECISION MAKING. These vignettes, taken together, form a narrative of my life. Serene Jones, the President of Union Theological Seminary in New York City, writes that discovering our core stories and reflecting on them is a form of theology. Though I would never pretend to be a theologian, my life does have, at its core, an interaction with religion. My striving to understand the gospel informed my life as a college administrator and teacher, and I trust has influenced the decisions I have made in these roles. While I would never argue that you have to be religious to be a good leader, the teachings of Jesus have been, for me, instructive. I have also interacted with leaders in India who were Hindus, and I have known leaders who were Muslim. Lou Silberman, a Jewish professor at Vanderbilt Divinity School, influenced me, and the writings of the Dalai Lama have informed me about the element of compassion. Faith, whether Christian, Muslim, Jewish, Hindu, Buddhist or other, provides important guidance and can serve as an anchor for leaders.

In writing my memoirs I have recalled various chapters in my life, and it has become clear that I never abandoned the calling to ministry I felt at the University of Virginia. I have wanted to engage in a vocation that used my skills to help other people. Even

Vanderbilt Chancellor Alexander Heard speaking at my inauguration on October 17, 1986.

Board of Trustees Chair Robert Frederick at my inauguration on October 17, 1986.

My family on my Inauguration Day.

DePauw graduate and former Unites States Vice President Dan Quayle at his inauguration on January 19, 1989.

With Former British Prime Minister Margaret Thatcher on April 7, 1992.

THE RT. HON. MARGARET THATCHER, O.M., F.R.S.

8th April, 1992

Dear Mr. Bottoms,

Thank you very much indeed for asking me to address the students and faculty of DePauw University yesterday. It was one of the largest audiences I have spoken to in the United States and I found the experience most stimulating. I am only sorry that I could not have stayed longer and met some of the young people who clearly are of high intellectual callibre, and appreciate the opportunities which your fine university affords them.

The lunch was delicious and I was delighted to meet your wife and the other guests at our table. It was a real treat to listen to the orchestra, choir and string trio. Please thank them very much on my behalf for entertaining us so well.

Altogether a delightful morning. My renewed thanks and very best wishes to you all.

I so much enjoyed the discussion we had.

All good wishes

Yours sincerely

Margaret Thatcher

Dr. Robert G. Bottoms.

Thank you letter from Margaret Thatcher, dated April 8, 1992 following her appearance as part of the Ubben Lecture Series.

Civil Rights leader and Depauw graduate Vernon Jordan at Commencement, May, 1993.

Former Secretary of State Colin Powell, Gwen and myself on November 2, 1994.

The Joyce Foundation Board of Directors, 1994. Pictured in the front row is Barack Obama.

Former First Lady Barbara Bush meets our dog, Bailey, after dinner at the President's Home, March 20, 1996.

Gwen, former British Prime Minister John Major and myself on October 29, 2001.

Duke University Basketball Coach Mike Krzyzewski, Gwen and myself on September 12, 2002.

The Holton Quadrangle, memorializing Phillip Holton for his $122 milion bequest to the university.

One of the duplexes built following the Rector fire of 2002.

The Janet Prindle Institute for Ethics dedicated in 2007.

Former Preisdent of the Soviet Union Mikhail
Gorbachev at his Ubben Lecture appearance,
October 27, 2005.

Taken at the Seabury Theological Seminary commencement in May
of 2009. (l-r) Episcopal Bishop of Chicago Jeff Lee, myself, Rev.
Gynne Wright, Seabury Board Chair, and Episcopal Bishop of New
York Andrew M.L. Dietsche.

Former British Prime Minister Tony Blair, Gwen and myself on March 3, 2008 at the President's home.

The Office of Tony Blair

From The Rt Hon Tony Blair

RECEIVED
MAR 2 1 2008

Dear Bob,

I really enjoyed my visit to DePauw last week.

Thank you and Gwen for hosting such a wonderful dinner at your home, it was kind and generous of you.

Best wishes,

your ever

Tony Blair

PO Box 60519
London
W2 7JU
www.tonyblairoffice.org

Note from PM Tony Blair written March 3, 2008 on the occasion of his visit to DePauw.

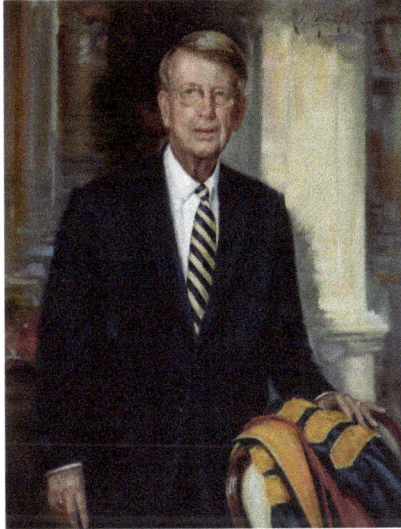

*Portrait that hangs in the Robert G.
Bottoms Alumni & Development Center,
dedicated on Oct. 12, 2018. The building is
depicted in the background.*

Dr. Robert G. Bottoms, the bulk of your distinguished working career was dedicated to the leadership and advancement of DePauw University. You joined the University in 1978 as vice president for university relations, you were later named executive vice president, and then in 1986 you were chosen as the 18th president of this institution, a role you held for an impressive 22 years. During your tenure at DePauw you led the drive for a far more diverse student body and faculty; advanced the study of the sciences, arts, and ethics on our campus; and spearheaded fundraising efforts in excess of half a billion dollars to make a DePauw education more meaningful and more accessible. With degrees from Birmingham-Southern College, Emory University, and Vanderbilt University you exemplify the drive for higher education and the quest for lifelong learning that also marks the DePauw experience. Your leadership of DePauw transformed our institution, and bettered us in ways we are only beginning to fully understand and appreciate.

For devoted, exemplary, and meritorious service to DePauw University, the **Old Gold Medal** is awarded to **Robert G. Bottoms,** 18th President of DePauw, by the University's Board of Trustees this 12th of October 2018.

Kathy Patterson Vrabeck
Board Chair

*Citation read by DePauw President, D.
Mark McCoy, upon my receiving the Old
Gold Medal, the highest honor bestowed from
DePauw University. October 12, 2018.*

The Old Gold Medal

though my education at Birmingham Southern College, Emory University and the Vanderbilt Divinity School caused me to leave the ministry, I nonetheless have sought to correct some injustices that need to be fixed. I have attempted, in some small way, to embrace minorities and those who are different.

Throughout my journey I have had an interesting relationship with the institutional church. I never could have survived as a Methodist minister—too many doubts and too much heresy. However, my seminary training left an indelible mark on my life. As I sought to nurture my own fundamental values, the theology I was exposed to at Emory and Vanderbilt illustrate the life of compassion I have sought to live. While I have achieved more professional success than expected from a modest boy from Sandusky, my career has been formed by the desire to serve. I have worked to secure scholarships for first-generation college students, and I have labored over the idealistic vision of developing an inclusive college community where white students, minority and international students could work together, learn from one another and live harmoniously within the community. This was my hope for DePauw—to bet on the future even though I never thought it would be easy and no results were guaranteed.

As I mentioned in Chapter One, in seminary I encountered the writings of Paul Tillich, Rudolf Bultmann and Dietrich Bonhoeffer. The image of Jesus portrayed by these writers presented quite a different picture from the Jesus of my adolescence. The exposure to contemporary theologians whetted my appetite for understanding, and for the last 50 years I have not stopped reading and studying.

Post seminary, I have been significantly influenced by Marcus Borg and the controversial Episcopal Bishop John Shelby Spong, both of whom were guest lecturers at DePauw. As I look back over my life, I have often been attracted to controversial figures. I recall attending a meeting of a few Methodist bishops and several presidents of Methodist Colleges in the mid 90's. The purpose of the meeting was to explore how Methodist colleges could make Methodism more attractive to students.

You can imagine how uneasy I was, but I did meet one bishop whom I genuinely liked. His name was Joseph Sprague, and he had an openness to pluralism that I appreciated. I came home and told Larry Burton, the pastor of Gobin Methodist Church on the campus, how much I liked Sprague. He laughed and told me Sprague was being tried for heresy. Exposure to these thinkers is how a fundamentalist boy from Sandusky developed into an elderly man with a liberal theology. I want to expand on this journey.

At Emory I began to outgrow my simple faith, but the life of Jesus continued to be a major influence. I studied his teachings, and it seemed to me his ministry might be summarized in one word—compassion. While I had many defining moments in my career, I struggled to let my behavior be governed by compassion for others: the black students who felt diminished by the ghetto party, the gay students who were offended by the anti-gay propaganda, and the women who were forced out of their sorority because of their physical appearance.

Many have written about how theology can be both negative and positive, and this certainly has been the case for me. Negative, because it undermined the naive beliefs that got in the way of my taking Jesus seriously, and positive in that it constructed a compelling vision of a compassionate way of living. I believe that salvation is not about the heaven and hell I was introduced to as a child. Nor is it about guaranteeing eternal life if we hold the correct beliefs. Rather, salvation is about a life that can be transformed into a life of service to others if one lives according to the teachings of Jesus. Christianity is about transforming oneself and the world. *An obsession with the afterlife is to neglect our responsibilities in this world.* Brian McLaren correctly admonishes those who make the gospel into an evacuation plan for the next world. The teachings of Jesus are seldom about the next life. They are more about day-to-day relationships. Jesus did not ask his followers to worship him. He pointed beyond himself. I learned from Paul Tillich that Jesus is the norm by which all goodness is judged, and we see through him to God. For me Jesus is the highest model of a compassionate life. Compassion was at the core of Jesus's ministry. It was a new ideal and stood over against the Old Testament God of retribution.

When I say a primary quality of the Christian life is compassion, I mean that in some ways the message of Jesus can be simple. It is about justice. In my experience with students and faculty and in my work addressing diversity and the teaching of ethics, a central question has always been: What does justice require? However, in many ways, justice and compassion are alien to the modern way of life. We tend to be competitive, individualistic and selfish, and these traits stand opposed to the message of Jesus.

While the message of compassion is sometimes portrayed in romantic ways to comfort people, I cannot escape the fact that Jesus was a troublemaker, and the teachings of Jesus are challenging. Columnist David Brooks has eloquently pointed out that in the Christian story it is not the accomplished but rather the poor who are close to God. The meek, the wounded, the lepers, and those who bear pain are the blessed ones. These teachings make me uncomfortable, and I believe that if you are not somewhat uncomfortable with the teachings of Jesus you have probably not understood them. Think about these concepts:

Blessed are the peacemakers.

Blessed are those who are persecuted for righteousness sake.

If you do not forgive, you will not be forgiven.

Love your enemies.

Be certain you are sinless before you cast the first stone.

Do not worship power and prestige and status. Become a servant.

Don't try to sit at the head of the table. Sit at the foot.

I cannot forget that, while Jesus lived a life of compassion, he had harsh words for some, especially the comfortable. There is an edginess to Christianity as we seek to follow a man who was executed by authorities. His persecutors were disturbed by Jesus's message of a new kind of kingdom built on compassion. In a world where religion was comfortable with culture, the message of Jesus challenged the establishment. Think about his practices. This man ate with tax collectors and sinners. He was charged with being a drunkard and a glutton. He defended a woman who washed his feet, and some of Jesus's actions elevated the status of women.

Unlike some contemporary preachers who promote a gospel of prosperity, Jesus did not see wealth as a gift from God. Rather he often saw it as idolatry. Recall the parable of the rich man who built barn after barn to house his wealth only to see his life end with no reward. Jesus said that it is easier for a camel to go through the eye of a needle than for a rich man to enter heaven. It is not so much that the wealthy are bad people, but the rich may find it difficult to imagine what life is like for those with few resources.

Most of Jesus's teachings are about how we are to live.

The religious life is not about dogma, but about living with actual people in real communities. In the Sermon on the Mount there are no words about what we are to believe, but there is a lot of instruction about what we are to do. Each Sunday we Episcopalians recite the Nicene Creed, which was written some 300 years after Jesus lived. But in the creed there are no words about what we are to do, only what we are to believe. A contemporary pastor, David Felten, observes that something has clearly gone wrong here. The church has too often concentrated on belief rather than action.

Comically, I can't imagine Saint Peter meeting me at the pearly gates when I die and asking me to explain the doctrine of the trinity or some theological dogma if I am to be permitted to enter heaven. Rather than question my theology, God is probably more interested in the way I lived rather than what I believed.

A meaningful life is not about believing certain things. It is about being a certain way. It is not about what we have, but who we are. To follow the teachings of Jesus is to cultivate a deep concern for the welfare of others. We are told to love our enemies, to care for the least of the people and that our greatest role is to be a servant. These teachings undermine theological arrogance and the point that to serve others is to experience the very presence of God. And we must see the humanity of people unlike ourselves. Jesus hung out with the wrong people. He literally touched the untouchable. But if we are left to our own instincts we tend to stick to our own kind. We live in communities with people like us. We like to go to school with people like us, and we often go to church with people just like us. Martin Luther King called 11:00 o'clock worship hour the most segregated hour in American society.

On the other hand Jesus embraced difference, the lepers, the Samaritans. I wonder who the Samaritans are in our society? The Muslims? The Blacks? The Latinos? The LGBTQ?

This way of thinking is so different from the individualistic theology that I grew up with—that Jesus saves. Jesus does save, but not from hell. Instead, following Jesus saves us from a life of trivial pursuits, from a life that misses the point, and from a life wasted on just living for ourselves. This whole concept of living for others has made a claim on me. You might say my life has been infected with the Jesus story. It haunts me to think about how I treat people who are unimportant by society's standards. As a college president I was challenged to be sensitive to the needs of minority students who sometimes found DePauw to be a hostile environment, and to minority faculty when some believed their presence was not earned but came about as a result of our Affirmative Action program. I worked to make the LGBTQ students feel included in the campus community, and I sought to stand against the elements of the Greek system that would judge people by the way they looked. I never publicly stated that my actions were a result of my faith, but this was undoubtedly the case.

In studying the life of Jesus numerous theologians have pointed out the tension between the intellect and some of the stories referenced in the gospels. I am referring to the virgin birth, the miracle stories and to a literal interpretation of the resurrection. While I value intellectual honesty, I do not think one has to believe in the literal interpretation of the New Testament stories to extract the larger meaning. After all, the scriptures are a product of human hands. Yet the historical criticism of the Bible does not necessarily lead to agnosticism. It can lead to a more intelligent and thoughtful faith. We are called to live a life of compassion, to stand by and for the oppressed, to listen empathetically and non-judgmentally to minorities and to be informed by their experiences. Even though it is mentally stimulating to debate theology and attempt to explain Christian dogma, we instead might focus on what Jesus did and what we can learn from it.

I believe Jesus is someone worth following, and he can be an anchor for our living in a secular age. Yet we live in difficult times to embrace compassion. Our government separates children from their immigrant parents and few seem to care. Racial tensions on college campuses indicate that we have not come far in eradicating prejudice. Many deny the science of climate change and seek to block attempts to stabilize the environment for our children and grandchildren. Income inequality is growing, not diminishing. In confronting these issues, it may seem idealistic to argue for lives of compassion, but this is the goal for which we should strive. We cannot be doomed to selfish existence.

I have attempted to share what I believe to be the essence of the gospel and my beliefs, which have evolved over 50 years. I have been privileged to study and work alongside theologians like Sallie McFague, Wilhelm Pauck, Peter Hodgson and Ed Farley. Were they to critique my writings about the life and teachings of Jesus, undoubtedly they would cast a critical eye. But what I have attempted to do is to narrate my personal journey of faith and expand on my own experience.

Clearly my faith influenced my life as a university administrator. As a college chaplain and later as a university president I was concerned about the young people growing up in today's society. So much has been written about secularization that I need not go into that here. I will simply observe how the world has changed since I grew up in the Sandusky Methodist Church. As a child there was nothing to do on Sunday morning but go to church. The church had no competition. There were no sports activities on Sundays. Not so today. The church has much competition. I was aware at Birmingham Southern, Vanderbilt and DePauw that a majority of young people come to college with no inclination to attend church and little knowledge of the Jesus narrative that has so influenced my life. Many students count on career and economic success for fulfillment. David Brooks called this belief the central illusion of our time. Studies show when students face moral dilemmas in college, they are quite likely to do what is most comfortable. They are exceedingly loyal to their friends, and it is very important to belong to the right group.

With this having been said, today's students do have many progressive beliefs. For example, research reveals that they have no objection to same sex marriage. As for the church, many see Christianity as irrelevant or worse, anti-gay, judgmental or simply old fashioned. Far too few have ever been exposed to a liberal or inclusive faith, and many have no knowledge of the life and teachings of Jesus.

Liberal arts colleges, particularly those that are church related, used to teach courses that dealt with basic beliefs, but today's research university model has given up on exploring the meaning of life. Harry R. Lewis, the controversial former Dean of Harvard College, has written that the fundamental job of undergraduate education is to help students grow up, to discover who they are, and to leave college as better human beings, determined to make the world a better place. Given the decline in the influence of the church, college is perhaps the best institution to engage young people in working for justice and goodness. When Bob Steele and I taught a course on leadership development, we wanted students to arrive at their own core values and decide how they would apply them after graduation.

We wanted students to see that college was about more than preparing for jobs and making money. There has to be more to life than this. A liberal arts education is the best opportunity young people have to explore the meaning of life, which is perhaps the most important question any person can contemplate. Given these beliefs and my seminary background, I wanted DePauw to address the students' need to deal with life's essential questions, and so we founded the Janet Prindle Institute for Ethics.

While nonreligious in nature, the Institute seeks to develop courses and programs to help students wrestle with contemporary issues and explore how compassion might guide an individual's decisions. Influenced by John Roth and Bob Steele, we wanted students to align their lives toward some ultimate good. We wanted DePauw to care as much for the development of a student's soul as for preparing them for well-paying jobs or graduate school. Many students have embraced the programs of the Institute, and the message of compassion seems to attract them without the props of traditional religious teachings. While I am somewhat critical of today's students, the work of the Institute indicates that, given the right setting, the call to a higher purpose in life still works.

Lest you think that my fascination with the life and teachings of Jesus has produced an easy path for my life, I want to correct the impression. When I observe the complexity of addressing institutional racism, rampant homelessness, and the stewardship of planet Earth, the teachings of Jesus seem somewhat naive. The sermons I hear often seem shallow and the words of the creeds ring hollow and irrelevant. In church I find myself admitting I do not believe all this stuff! The idea of a literal devil is not believable to me, and I am uncomfortable with any minister who has the audacity to say he or she speaks for God. Observing all the hurt in the world, I have even, at times, questioned the existence of God. However I am reminded that no less a servant than Mother Teresa had doubts. In her memoirs she wrote that there was a time when she felt torn between having lost God and having the unquenchable desire to reach Him. So, in these times of doubt, I have come to think it is not so much what one believes, but how one lives. In terms of knowing God and understanding theological dogma, I remain agnostic—a state of not knowing, but nonetheless attracted to the teachings of Jesus. You might say I have learned to trust God without certainty. I know what I have come to believe, but I do not know that I am right. For that matter, how can any of us know we are right? If we are honest, we cannot. We can use our intellect and be in dialogue with the teachings of Jesus, but living a compassionate life is rarely easy.

While I used to think Christianity was about believing, I now think of it as a journey. What T.S. Eliot wrote about the church is also true about the individual:

"And the church must be forever building,

and always decaying

And always restored."

So why be Christian? The life of Jesus models a path to follow. And by following Jesus I do not mean just trooping along after him, but honestly trying to live a compassionate life. Other leaders may choose to follow different religions or no religion at all, but the Christian tradition has been a home for me, and I appreciate its wisdom. I find the Eucharist especially meaningful. In spite of all my doubts, there is something about sharing a meal with the diverse people who gather at the table to recall the life and teachings of Jesus. Like Marcus Borg wrote in his final book before his death, at age 75, I primarily feel gratitude for the life I have lived, for the memories of my childhood, for the various conversions I have undergone, and for the convictions I now hold. I have outgrown my youthful faith in Jesus, but he remains the one who has most influenced my life. While I could never put into words a coherent and full explanation of Jesus's life I will always remember the words of Albert Schweitzer which he wrote in *The Quest for the Historical Jesus*:

"He comes to us as One unknown, without a name, as of old, by the lakeside, He came to those men who knew Him not. He speaks to us the same word: 'Follow thou me!' and sets us to the tasks which he has to fulfill for our time. He commands. And to those who obey Him, whether they be wise or simple, He will reveal Himself in the toils, the conflicts, the sufferings which they shall pass through in His fellowship, and, as an ineffable mystery, they shall learn in their own experience who he is."

Before closing this chapter, I want to expand on a subject I mentioned earlier—one that is of interest to anyone my age. What happens to us when we die? Because of my work with students I was attracted to Harvey Cox's book, *When Jesus Came to Harvard*. At Harvard Cox taught an undergraduate class called "Jesus and the Moral Life." The course became so popular that the lectures had to be held in a large theater. In the first couple of years of teaching the course, Cox stopped at the crucifixion and dodged any consideration of the Easter story. But after a year or two he began to have a heavy conscience about omitting the Biblical account of Easter. Even the most critical scholars admit that the scattered and dispirited followers did experience something after the crucifixion that convinced them death had not finished Jesus for good. They ran the risk of arrest and death because, as they said time and time again, they had experienced Jesus in their midst. "Jesus Christ is risen" means that Jesus lives in the lives of those who followed him and the cause of Jesus moves on. This is what the gospel writers attempted to convey in their contradictory stories of their encounters with him. Hope, not belief, is what the stories attempt to convey.

I remain agnostic about a literal interpretation of the resurrection and the promise it gives for a life after death, but I can hope that this world is not the final conclusion. To be sure, death is the defining theological moment in everyone's life. After surviving a heart attack two years ago, I was in the Intensive Care Unit of St. Mary's Hospital. Awake in the wee hours of the morning, I lay in the bed with wires and tubes running all over my body. It dawned on me that I could die…even die that morning. Interestingly enough I was not afraid. Nor did I have any understanding of what would happen to me if I died. I just had to wonder: what would death be like? A new adventure or not? While I have doubts about being greeted by Saint Peter and a host of angels, I have no idea what life after death will be like. I will just have to leave that up to God.

My hospital experience reminded me that as a young boy, I recall laying on my back in our front yard and gazing into the sky. I wondered exactly where heaven was. I wondered how it was that I had ended up here. And I wondered what might happen when I died. Today, after years of study and reflection I must confess that no one knows. It will simply happen.

Throughout my life I have learned a lot from other people, especially writers and thinkers more sophisticated and original than I. When at DePauw I worked all summer on my opening remarks to the faculty. Generally they responded in a positive way—sort of, "Tell us what you read this summer." I would take what I learned from others, infuse it with my own experience, and pass it along. And in a way that is what I have done with this chapter on compassion. Many of my beliefs are unconventional, but as I reach the sunset years of my life, I realize that I have generally been one who thought differently from other people. I seemed to see the world as a contrarian. Perhaps this is why I have been attracted to the teachings of Jesus. His life stands over against many of the practices we may choose, but it centers on the ideal of compassion and how that concept has the power to transform individuals and society. So, what do we know for certain? That we should love one another and treat others as we wish to be treated. And that we take care of the least of these. But this love is hard. Robert Michael Franklin of the Candler School of Theology reminds us that loving all our brothers and sisters takes every ounce of courage and compassion we have in our bodies.

❧

CHAPTER FIVE

LEADERSHIP LESSONS LEARNED

WHEN I BEGAN THIS BOOK I HAD TWO GOALS IN MIND. First I wanted it to be a memoir of my life. Second, I wanted to write about leadership lessons learned during my career as a Methodist minister and later as a college administrator. My purpose in addressing leadership is not to offer groundbreaking insights, but to simply shed light on leadership theory and illustrate leadership as a practitioner.

My experience as a leader involves four institutions of higher education: Birmingham Southern College, Vanderbilt University, DePauw University and Seabury Western Theological Seminary. I learned a great deal about leadership from my three decades with the Joyce Foundation in Chicago, a ten year stint on the Posse Foundation Board in New York City, and many years of service on the Board of the Center for Leadership Development in Indianapolis. I also spent two years as a consultant to the Lilly Endowment, evaluating their grants to theological education. From these experiences I observed many different styles of leadership,

During my years as president of DePauw I also interacted with many successful business leaders, most of whom were trustees of the university. They include Ian Rolland of Lincoln National Corporation, Tim Solso of Cummins Engine, Judson Green of the Walt Disney Company and Navteq, Robert Frederick of RCA,

Tim Ubben of Lincoln Capital Management, Stuart Watson of Heublein Liquors, David Hoover and John Fisher of Ball Brothers Corporation, Richard Wood of Eli Lilly, Nicholas Chabraja of General Dynamics, and James Stewart, the Pulitzer Prize winning author. While this list is not meant to be exhaustive, it is indicative of the caliber of people who worked alongside me. These people modeled good leadership and provided me with insights as to how to lead the university.

To be certain, studying leadership and writing about it is much easier than leading a diverse organization like a college or university, but I had numerous mentors and much good fortune along the way. Obtaining a scholarship to the Engineering School at the University of Virginia was formative for me. It opened a whole new world for an awkward boy from Sandusky and set me out on a new vocational path. Attending Birmingham Southern and studying under Max Miller prepared me for my academic work at Emory, and my time as a student and later as an administrator at Vanderbilt Divinity School made me into the person I have become. I also had several jobs that contributed to my development as a leader. I was fortunate to work at Birmingham Southern both as chaplain and as a development officer, which created a path out of the formal ministry and into college administration.

At Vanderbilt I met Robert Nelson, who taught me about

development, and who remained a mentor for my first 25 years at DePauw. At DePauw I met many successful leaders through the Ubben Lecture Series and I learned from them. I also benefited from the many black guests we had at the university to help us with our diversity emphasis. People like Roger Wilkins, Carl Rowan, Cornel West and Vernon Jordan helped me understand the black experience and how to strategize to make DePauw more inclusive. I even had the opportunity to work with Barack Obama when we served on the Joyce Foundation Board together. In short, I have been very fortunate. I received a good education, had many challenging jobs and with them the opportunity to interact with numerous leaders. If I view my life as a story to be told, the storyline is one of gratitude.

One of the primary attributes of a leader is to have a clear vision of where one's organization needs to go. My goal was to make DePauw a better place, and to do so I had three main objectives. We had a long history of excellence in science education, and I sought to build on this by securing funds for a new biology building. Second, we were a predominantly white institution, and I initiated the effort to attract minority students and faculty. Finally I wanted to enhance our ability to help students find a direction for their lives, hence the establishment of the Janet Prindle Institute for Ethics. During the years of my presidency there were many opportunities for distraction. I observed several presidential colleagues whose vision for their institution included many, and perhaps all, of the good ideas brought forth by the community. *But I was never seduced by the temptation to have dozens of goals.* Instead I remained true to what was needed to accomplish my three emphases.

With a clear vision of what I hoped to accomplish, I set out to secure faculty support. The leader of any university must be able to persuade an often unruly group of people from various disciplines with conflicting loyalties to support a common vision. We established a University Priorities Committee, a group of faculty elected from across disciplines, and I used them to assist in strategic planning. I advanced my own ideas, but I listened to faculty criticisms and concerns. Gaining support for science education was easy because Harrison Hall, which housed the Biology Department, was badly in need of repair. On the surface the faculty also supported the idea of racial diversification. Resistance only came when we began to act and not just talk. The third emphasis, helping the students form basic values, had some opposition because no one wanted to project their values onto the students. But I spoke often about these three goals, and no one questioned where I wanted to lead the institution. I also listened to the faculty about practical concerns. Even with the sensitive issue of faculty pay we cooperated. While the administration set the faculty salary pool, I allowed the Priorities Committee to decide how the pool was to be divided.

In terms of leadership lessons learned, I first established a clear vision, one that was built on our previous strengths, and one that was achievable if proper time and resources were made available. In hindsight, I believe I was able to work with faculty because I had so much admiration for them. My standard for excellence had been learned both from my professors at Birmingham Southern and Emory University as well as Alexander Heard, the Chancellor of Vanderbilt University when I worked there. While my predecessor often had conflicts with the faculty, I respected them and projected onto them the admiration I had for my professors who did so much to mold me. I worked on the assumption that the faculty at DePauw interacted with students the way my professors interacted with me—caring about the individual and setting high academic standards.

Given my experiences with faculty, what I coveted for the students was an education that aligned their lives toward some goal. I fundamentally believed that during the course of my career colleges and universities had become more diverse, more pluralistic and more specialized, to the exclusion of exposing students to ideals for how to live their lives. As David Brooks has pointed out, universities may have become information rich and meaning poor. I wanted to avoid this tendency at DePauw.

Helping students find meaning for their lives should have been a natural goal for DePauw. We had been founded by the

Methodists. The first 16 presidents of DePauw had been Methodist clergy, and Gobin Memorial Church rested on a prominent corner of the campus. For decades, numerous faculty and students had been active there. However, by the time I had assumed the presidency, Gobin was less a force on the campus than it had been in the past. Fewer faculty participated and our students were less inclined to attend church than in earlier times. The Methodist chaplaincy had also become impotent for a majority of our students, although we did have a significant number of students involved in community service. While these traditions formed an important ingredient of our past, the establishment of the Janet Prindle Institute for Ethics seemed to be an extension and expansion of our heritage. It aims to help students identify fundamental values and provide avenues to improve society.

To promote my vision for the university I worked with the admissions office to market the institution. We wanted to be clear on what we were and what we were not, never pretending to be all things to all people. I wanted us to offer something hard to come by, a commitment to the big idea of having students identify their core values as they interacted with the faculty. As the prospective student market changed, selling DePauw was a constant challenge. Students had no allegiance to any particular type of institution, large or small, independent or state supported. In this evolving environment I wanted DePauw to emphatically state who we were.

We were distinctively Midwestern although we could meet the academic needs of students from anywhere. Indianapolis, Chicago, Detroit, St. Louis and Louisville were key cities for us. We sought to market DePauw as a different kind of place. I wanted us to offer a liberal arts education with internship possibilities and an international component, combined with a desire to discover the values one wants to promote after college. Thus, we believed we were offering something others were not. While this vision might not appeal to everyone, we were determined to be true to ourselves and our traditions.

If clarity of vision was the first leadership trait I promoted, cultivating what some have called "emotional intelligence" was also paramount. There are two kinds of intelligence: intellectual and emotional. While I never thought of myself as being the brightest person at the university, I did think of myself as having emotional intelligence. I had the ability to recognize my own feelings and those of others. *I could motivate others, and I sought out and befriended the marginalized.* I believed it was important to have as large a tent as possible, and that we would only strengthen the institution by listening to all voices, as long as we did not betray our essential nature.

Creating a clear vision and cultivating emotional intelligence are certainly key attributes of a leader. But there are others.

Most leaders are very busy, and as I wrote in Chapter Two, it is important to spend some time in solitary reflection, forcing oneself to withdraw from the daily demands so as not to drift away from one's values and vision. I built into my schedule some time each week for uninterrupted reflection. How were we progressing on accomplishing our goals? What forces were helping? Were there destructive forces, and if so what was the source of discontent? While most of my structured reflections were spent sitting alone in my study, I also benefited from spending time at our home on the shores of Lake Monroe in Bloomington, Indiana. Often I felt the need to get away from the campus, sit on the porch overlooking the lake and just think. Rather than seeking a physical getaway, some leaders in other institutions used their reflective time to write in a journal. I never attempted this, but now I wish I had because so many details have eluded me as I think about my 30 years at DePauw. Whether a leader keeps a journal or not, reflection gives the brain an opportunity to pause amidst the busyness and sort through experiences. The exercise of reflection causes one to do something we typically do not like to do—to slow down and adopt the mindset of possibly not knowing.

One image I found helpful was developed by Ronald Heifetz of the Harvard Business School. Imagine you are at a party. As you move through a crowded room, everyone seems to be having a good time. Some are dancing and others are engaged in polite conversation. But if you exit the room and assume a place on the balcony, you can see everyone from a different vantage point. Do some people seem to be isolated? Some disengaged? You can gain a totally different perspective on the balcony, as opposed to standing in the middle of a crowded room. A helpful image for a leader is to imagine being on the balcony and observing, rather than being at the center of the party with so many distractions.

If we do not have a well-defined vision and clarity of values, the cynics will bring us to our knees. When I speak of core values I mean a way of believing what we hold to be the most important. I have led classes on leadership for numerous churches, the College for Bishops of the Episcopal Church, the Consortium for Endowed Parishes of the Episcopal Church and an MBA course at Piedmont College. While I never tried to impose my two defining values— compassion and intellectual honesty—on other people I worked to assist people, to discover their own.

I used the following exercise in class. Participants were asked to make a list of values they admire. Examples are authenticity, balance, love, family, honesty, humility, generosity, etc. Sometimes the list is quite long. I then ask the students to begin eliminating values until they can get down to the two most defining values for them. I have arbitrarily chosen two because I believe that if you have more than two values that define who you are, you really have no priorities. Once you have arrived at two, ask yourself, does this define me?

There is tremendous freedom in defining one's basic values and then living them out. As I wrote earlier, I discovered my two values when my father demanded of me, the young minister, to tell him what would happen to him when he died. I wanted to be compassionate but I also had to be intellectually honest and so I admitted I did not know. These two values—compassion and intellectual honesty—informed the rest of my life.

I recall one instance in my life that illustrates this. Then Vice President Dan Quayle, an alumnus of DePauw, was speaking at the institution to a crowd of several thousand. In his speech he defended his and President George H.W. Bush's misgivings about Affirmative Action. Most of the crowd applauded, but I remained seated with my arms folded. I was later told by a black faculty member that every black person in the audience noticed that I did not applaud the Vice President, even though he was a guest of the university. Amidst all the voices we hear we must wonder: what are my essential values saying now? You have to ignore critical voices when they are destructive, even though you feel comfortable with multiple voices. With all the voices that compete for your attention, you know you are immersed in your values when the decisions are tough. Doing the right thing is rarely easy.

The good leader focuses on vision, and keeps the focus there in the face of the temptation to wander. The so-called "cognitive control" enables one to pursue a vision despite distractions and setbacks. A leader may sometimes arrive at the office with a clear plan for the day, encounter many disruptions, and then on the way home realize only a few priorities have been addressed. Trivial demands take away from the real work that needs to be done. Being clear on values and vision has many practical benefits. Such clarity can even allow one to turn down a job offer that might be tempting financially, but does not fit with one's principles and long term goals. This happened to me twice. Being self-aware means having a deep understanding of one's emotions, strengths, weaknesses, needs and drives. People with self-awareness are neither overly critical nor unrealistically hopeful. Rather, they are honest with themselves.

In developing my leadership skills I benefited from being an avid reader of the *Harvard Business Review*. By engaging with their many publications on leadership, I chose not to emulate others, but rather to integrate their insights with my own experience. I sought to face troubles without being troubled. When I became anxious I sought to be relaxed emotionally—a sort of happy warrior. People are uncomfortable with uncertainty and they seek a leader who is calm, clear-headed and at times even courageous.

I also believe a good leader needs to possess excellent persuasive skills, be a good speaker and always be well-prepared. I learned this lesson early in my career. I was in my second year as the Associate Pastor of the First Methodist Church in Birmingham, Alabama. Edwin Kimbrough, the Senior Pastor, had spoken several times to our bishop, W. Kenneth Goodson, to convince him I was a gifted preacher. One Sunday evening, just after attending the week-long annual conference of the church, Bishop Goodson slipped into the evening worship service to hear me speak. Because I had been at the annual conference each day, I did not have the usual time to prepare my sermon. In short, it was awful and here was the bishop listening to me stumble through my remarks. While nothing was ever said to me directly, I was humiliated. I vowed never to be unprepared for speaking again. And I was not! In my comments to the Board of Trustees, the Faculty Institute, gatherings of prospective students and the annual alumni convocation I was, if anything, overly prepared thanks to my experience with the bishop. One word of caution however: you can never allow your speaking ability to cover up the shallowness of the argument. *Form must not trump substance.* Again I learned this at First Methodist, when many parishioners who praised my sermons voted against allowing black students to enter our kindergarten.

A good leader also must have a steady presence. You cannot show up as one person one day and another the next. You must also develop the skill of remaining calm when confronted with tension. There was one instance when two boys in a pickup truck drove through the campus and yelled racist remarks at black students on the sidewalk. The campus community was understandably enraged and some faculty and students began to organize a march to City Hall supposedly to "reclaim our city." I hesitated to encourage this even though I had participated in a march for racial justice after the ghetto party.

After a few days of investigation by the campus police, it was determined that the culprits were not even from Greencastle, so a march to City Hall would have been inappropriate. In a time of tension it is important to obtain all the facts rather than get swept up in the emotions of the moment. These moments that challenge can also teach us about leading effectively. But it is not enough to remain calm in the face of tension. You must also be very careful about *what* you say. People do listen and you are "on" twenty four hours a day.

I have also learned that good leaders need a support team to stay on course, especially in difficult times. No leader can accomplish significant goals alone. Support may come from spouses, mentors or colleagues. Leaders need feedback from their support people, even if it is unpleasant. If we shield ourselves from feedback we quit growing. Surrounding oneself with "yes" people is counterproductive. However, honest feedback is sometimes difficult because it strikes at two core needs: the need to learn and grow and the need to be accepted the way you are. Too often seeking feedback is seen as a sign of weakness. It does take some humility to accept the fact that we have something to learn.

Another observation about leadership is the need to be transparent. My predecessor had a running battle with *The DePauw* newspaper and its cadre of students who viewed themselves as investigative reporters. I determined early in my presidency to be as cooperative as possible with the student journalists. I made it a practice to give the editor of the paper a thirty-minute interview each Monday morning. During that time I was willing to answer any and all questions, except those pertaining to sensitive personnel issues. Jack McWethy, a highly respected reporter for ABC News, spent a week on campus advising the newspaper. Jack was a former editor of *The DePauw,* and by his own admission, had been a thorn in the flesh of the president. At the end of his week on campus, Jack came to me with a question: how was it that the newspaper reporters were so kind to me? Undoubtedly it was because I was transparent to them and held these weekly briefing sessions.

In attempting to cite leadership lessons learned throughout my career, I write with some humility because I have, no doubt, benefited from white privilege. White people have been raised in communities where we were taught racial superiority and this went largely unchallenged by anyone. I resonate with Peggy McIntosh of Wellesley College who writes about white privilege. I can go shopping well assured that I will not be followed or harassed. I can turn on the television or read a newspaper and see my people widely represented. I can find music of my race in a music store. I never had to educate our children to be aware of systemic racism for their own daily safety. I can take a job with an Affirmative Action employer without having co-workers suspect I got it because of my race. In learning about white privilege I have benefited from my friendship with the many black guests who helped with our diversity initiative.

My sensitivity to white privilege and issues of race was no doubt enhanced by my time at Vanderbilt University, which had a long history of dealing with race. Vanderbilt was integrated in 1962, and was the first university in the South to do so, thus escaping its image as a southern finishing school. After blacks were admitted, one student in the Divinity School became active in training blacks to nonviolently desegregate the lunch counters in Nashville. This upset many conservative members of the Board of Trust and the black student, James Lawson, was expelled. The faculty of the Divinity School resigned en masse as a protest. And then they were joined by several members of the Medical School, who also threatened to resign if Lawson was not reinstated. These actions by faculty caused the Board of Trust to reverse itself, and Lawson was readmitted. Vanderbilt thus positioned itself as a private university in the Deep South that stood for racial justice, and this ethos permeated the university both while I was a student and then as an administrator in the Divinity School. As an alumnus of Vanderbilt I came to realize how the struggle to survive white supremacy was a full-time job.

I was also exposed to racial injustice at the First United Methodist Church in Birmingham where I had to face the hypocrisy of whites who could not come close to practicing the Golden Rule. I worked with white clergy who spoke often about racial prejudice, but did little to diminish it. I am reminded of James Cone's quote from W.E.B. Dubois, who said, "If Jesus came today, he would eat with the Negro and seldom see the interior of St. John the Divine."

I realize how truly difficult it is for me, as a white person, to step in a black person's shoes. James Cone has written eloquently about how the memory of lynching Negroes has scarred the memory of an entire race. Cone documents that there have been over 5,000 lynchings, and in its heyday these were often public spectacles announced in the newspapers and attended by large crowds. Black people were lynched for something as simple as walking too close to a white woman, and these lynchings communicated that blacks could not be safe, as no one would protect them. They were at risk all the time. As a white man, I have never had to overcome such a tragic memory.

During my career at DePauw, there were many days when I felt great, even like a good leader. The trappings of the office contributed to this. The academic regalia, wearing the presidential medallion, and speaking to large crowds on opening day and commencement all seemed to say that I was important. It was unusual for a boy from humble origins to have the opportunity to host a dinner for Tony Blair and hear him defend entry into the war against Iraq, to lunch with Margaret Thatcher and listen to her compare the admiration she had for Ronald Reagan with her doubts about the ability of George H.W. Bush, and to introduce Mikael Gorbachev to our students and hear him discuss world hunger and how nations must learn to share resources. I courted millionaires and occasionally billionaires to win their support of the university.

But there were other days when I felt like an impostor. Many writers in the *Harvard Business Review* helped me realize that leaders often experience this "Impostor Syndrome." In fact, one study found that being discovered as incompetent was the number one fear of executives worldwide. Perhaps it began when I, in my green gabardine suit at a University of Virginia fraternity party, felt so out of place. Being able to identify these feelings and recognize them for what they are has been of significant benefit to me.

Good leaders, at some point, must prepare for their eventual transition. This was certainly true in the emphasis I had placed on diversity at DePauw. Early on I realized that it was not enough to have minority students and faculty. No, the governance structure of DePauw also needed to be impacted. I worked hard to make the Alumni Board, the Board of Visitors and the Board of Trustees representative of DePauw's new reality. Outstanding blacks and Hispanics were recruited and they rose to leadership positions. I took great pride in seeing the first black person and the first Hispanic person become Presidents of the Alumni Association. And this was done, not by my request, but by the Alumni Association itself which had come to recognize the talents of minority members in the alumni body. After 22 years as president I had come to realize that DePauw could never go back to being basically an all-white institution. And I counted this as one of my most significant achievements.

As I approach the last chapter of my life I realize how important institutions have been. The church helped form me and universities broadened me. Today both institutions are challenged. The church has lost much of its influence and universities have become so specialized and job oriented that the liberal arts education which benefited me has become suspect.

In conclusion, I have served two presidencies. What has made me successful at work? No doubt chance has played a major role. I was fortunate to be offered the job as chaplain of Birmingham Southern College just as I was trying to decide what to do with my life. Similarly, when Joe Sparks recommended me for the job at Vanderbilt, I was able to begin to learn how to be a university administrator. By chance Bob Nelson was assigned to Vanderbilt Divinity School as a development consultant, and he became a mentor for decades. Finally, it was by chance that the job at DePauw became available at the exact time I had decided to leave the large university setting at Vanderbilt. I never could have imagined working for a college with so much latent promise and whose values matched so well with mine.

For certain, I have been very fortunate, but I have also worked hard. I learned to work hard: cutting grass at age 14, selling clothes at Newberry's Department Store while in high school, running a blowtorch at Birmingham Rail and Locomotive, working in the library at Emory and unloading packages on the night shift at United Parcel while I was a student at Emory.

I never thought of myself as particularly liberal, and I tried to see all sides of an issue. Perhaps one of my greatest assets was that I could get along with the conservatives on the Board of Trustees while pushing a progressive agenda. In the initial days of our advocacy for diversity one older trustee told me he knew I was right, but this was just not the DePauw so many had come to love. Yet we persevered and the university became stronger and more relevant.

How do I want to be remembered? As one that made a good institution even better. I have enjoyed some success, but I have also had my detractors. Upon my retirement, one local Greencastle resident stated that I never met a liberal cause I didn't embrace.

Still, it is what it is. As my life approaches the sunset years, I have come to believe that a substantial legacy is arguably the most powerful thing you can pass on to others. It allows you to have influence well into the future.

Perhaps my legacy is that DePauw is certainly a more diverse place; the Prindle Institute is flourishing and Bexley Seabury is serving the needs of the Episcopal Church. The Posse Foundation continues to meet the needs of hundreds of minority students each year, and finally I still hear from students whose lives were positively influenced by DePauw University. Tim and Sharon Ubben gave DePauw a lovely new facility for the alumni and development staff and they placed my name on it. I feel I have lived a life "well spent," and I leave a legacy that I hope has touched others in a positive way.

❧

EPILOGUE

W RITING THIS MEMOIR HAS CAUSED ME TO EXAMINE HOW MY LIFE CHANGED OVER TIME. For the first twenty or so years of my life I accepted things as they were. Society, though segregated, had been good to me. It was through the liberal arts education at Birmingham Southern College and graduate school at Emory and Vanderbilt Universities that I slowly began to see the world in an expanded way. I was most fortunate to wind up at DePauw, an institution whose history coincided with my values. In reflecting back over the years of my presidency two contributions stand out. The success we had in diversifying the student body and faculty changed the institution forever. I well remember the reaction to my inauguration speech, when I declared diversity to be one of my goals. Many of my college president friends secretly told me I had made a mistake. Everyone supposedly knew that minority students and faculty would never come to a college in rural Indiana. But we proved them wrong.

The second lasting accomplishment was the founding of the Jane Prindle Institute for Ethics. Based on my background, I had always understood education to be a moral endeavor. At DePauw, where the early presidents taught a capstone course for seniors dealing with what constitutes the good life, it only seemed natural to provide a place central to the college where issues of morality could be raised. And it was important to me that the Institute have a building of its own with an endowment for programming, a sort of insurance policy for the future, guaranteeing that no future president or faculty could minimize the institutional emphasis on ethics.

❧

APPENDIX I

WHAT IT IS TO BE A COLLEGE PRESIDENT

To labor constantly for the world with no thought of self, to find indifference and opposition where you ought to have active assistance, to meet criticism with patience and the open attacks of ignorance without resentment, to plead with others for their own good, to follow sleepless nights with days of incessant toil, to strive continuously with ever attaining—this it is to be a college president. But this is only half the truth. To be associated with ambitious youth and high-minded men, to live in an atmosphere charged with thoughts of the world's greatest thinkers, to dream of a golden age not in the past but in the future and to have the exalted privilege of striving to make that dream a reality, to build up great kingdoms of material conquest and make daily life richer and fuller, to spiritualize wealth and convert it into weal, to enrich personal character and elevate all human relationships, to leave the impress of one's life on a great and immortal institution—this, too, it is to be a college president.

Chancellor James H. Kirkland
Vanderbilt University (1909)

Recreation of the plaque given to me upon my inauguration as the Eighteenth President of DePauw University, October 17, 1986.

Appendix II

Inauguration Address

By

President Robert G. Bottoms

Depauw University

At A Dinner For The University's Faculty

October 16, 1986

ONE COULD HARDLY SAY ENOUGH ABOUT THE STRENGTH OF DEPAUW UNIVERSITY TODAY. In this, our Sesquicentennial year, we are completing the most successful fund-raising campaign any private liberal arts college in this country has ever attempted. Current gifts and commitments to our Sesquicentennial Campaign total in excess of $109 million.

Alumni support in the past two decades has enabled us to erect the Performing Arts Center, the Julian Mathematics Center, the Lilly Physical Education and Recreation Center; to restore East College; to renovate Asbury Hall; and current plans call for a renovation of Harrison Hall. Certainly we have facilities which enable us to support the most ambitious academic progress.

However, it is our <u>people</u> in the person of an increasingly skilled students body and a richly competent faculty which will continue to sustain us in the future.

With all these strengths a new president of DePauw faces several questions: What do we lack? What keeps DePauw from claiming its rightful place as one of the premier undergraduate institutions in the country? What outstanding opportunities are afforded us as we address the challenges in American culture?

Let me review what I have already raised for the faculty as a concern. The question revolves around the issue of whether or not DePauw is reflective of the society which we seek to serve. I am talking about the issue of diversity.

The facts are these. The Hispanic segment of the United States population is the fastest growing part of America. Asians constitute the second fastest growing population segment, blacks third, and finally, the Caucasians consist of the fourth fastest growing segment of our population. The largest twenty-four school systems in the United States today have what demographers call "a minority majority." Twenty-seven percent of the high school students in America today are, in fact, minorities.

By the year 2010, one out of every three Americans will either be black, Hispanic or Asian. Mexican-American women today average bearing 2.9 children per person; black women, 2.4 per person. Caucasian women are reproducing at a rate of 1.7 children per person and demographers inform us that it takes an average of 2.1 children per woman just to stay even in sustaining one's population. (It might also be noted in the so-called "baby boom" white women were reproducing approximately 2.9 children per person.).

So what are we to make of all this? One of the things Harold

Hodgkinson points out in a paper called "Diversity Is Our Middle Name," is that institutions in the heartland, like Indiana, are obviously much less affected by these demographic trends than those people in California and New York, Texas, Florida, and Michigan. Yet perhaps the most important implication for us is that the nation in which our students will live will be more ethnically diverse than it has even been, and we have to wonder if campus culture can reflect just what this diversity means.

Hodgkinson contends that there are still colleges in the country (although certainly not DePauw) where Spanish language and literature are perceived to be second rate and the outstanding students are steered to the more established programs in German and French. We have to wonder if one of the challenges before us is not to allow our curriculum to begin to show a parity for the new cultural links to South America and Asia. How will DePauw be relevant to the young people growing up in this diverse culture? Many contemporary students are more familiar, Hodgkinson says, with European culture than with life in the Bronx or Chicago's South Side. It's a bit disarming, and we wonder if we are prepared for this phenomenon.

The issue I am raising is not of one survival – DePauw most certainly will survive. The question I raise is one of significance. The welfare of our nation and the concept of justice both demand that DePauw cannot be irrelevant to one-third of our population.

Given these current population trends, one has to wonder how DePauw is performing vis-à-vis premier liberal arts institutions in the Midwest. Quite frankly, the picture is not too complimentary. DePauw has the highest proportion of Caucasian students of any of the Great Lakes Colleges Association consortium. Of the nineteen private liberal arts colleges in Indiana as listed in a September issue of *The Chronicle of Higher Education*, DePauw ranks seventeenth, having twenty percent fewer minorities in our student population than we had five years ago. We need to force ourselves to reflect on what this means. What, for example, does it mean to graduate our student body today with little or no exposure to people or cultures that are different? Do our students know and understand the current roles of Latin America, Asia, and Africa?

Frank F. Wong, Vice President for Academic Affairs at Beloit College in Wisconsin, wrote in *Liberal Education* in the spring of 1985, pointing out that we live in a world and a time where cultures are in constant contact and conflict with one another. He states, "We are all <u>pilgrims</u> on a journey to seek truth, but we are also all <u>immigrants</u> in a new and not very familiar land where the signposts of the past may not be the signposts of the present or the future."

Dr. Wong notes that in higher education today we are experiencing a "back to basics" movement, indicating that we in higher education have perhaps lost our traditional anchors. The public has accepted this argument. Secretary of Education Bennett has pointed out that we must first learn to know ourselves and only then can we face the world in confidence. But there is a problem with such thinking. While we may live in the midst of a "return to basics philosophy," the world has changed. It is no longer the Western-dominated world with which we had learned to deal. Given the emergence of the Eastern and Latin American nations, can the true pilgrim today be content with a journey through western classics alone? Would not our perspective on enduring issues be more universal if we included in our core programs not only classics of the western traditions but other traditions as well?

As Americans, we are familiar with the phenomenon which makes it easy for us to leave the rest of the world behind us. We are concerned with what affects us locally, our neighborhood, the cities in which we live, the local community. Yet we are entering an era in which the world has experienced a major departure from the Euro-centered world of the late 19th century.

Dr. Wong reminds us of a recent folk ballad in which a young man depicts his girlfriend as wearing jeans made in France, shoes made in Spain, driving a car made in Japan, and he laments at least she was made in the U.S.A.

An indication of how small and interrelated the world

community has become is the fact that only a couple of weeks ago I sat with a planning group of people in Greencastle, Indiana, to help formulate a plan to bring Japanese industry to Greencastle. Successful strategies had already been developed in such small Midwestern towns as Columbus, Indiana, and Rushville, Indiana. Who would have predicted such conversations twenty years ago?

As Frank Wong suggests, we truly have become both pilgrims and immigrants. Too long, perhaps, we have been "intellectual tourists and sightseers." We have traveled through foreign cultures but chose not to engage them.

We have to wonder if such an experience adequately prepares our students to live in the ethnically-diverse world in which they will find themselves. Dare we not explore a program of visiting professors to expose our students to the best of thinking of other cultures? In our lectureship program, do we not want to expose our students to the in-depth thinking represented by a world foreign to Greencastle? Given the present world situation, is it adequate for us to allow our international education program to continue sending our students primarily to France, Frieburg, Athens and London? Can we be content in this time to continue our gradual movement toward an all-white student body? To be educationally relevant and viable in the world community we have to courageously and seriously explore the issue of diversity in the student body, in the faculty and in the curriculum.

II.

If we have an opportunity in exploring the diversity issue, we have no less opportunity in addressing ourselves to the status of science education in America.

John Schafer, the current president of Research Corporation for Scientific Advancement, reminded all the presidents of the so-called "Oberlin Conference Colleges" that even though the United States has double the population of Japan, we are producing half as many scientists. Last year, of the 1,100 Ph.D's produced in physics in this country, one-half were foreign born and sought to return to their home countries. In less than three years the same fate will face us in chemistry.

National Merit Scholars have long been the source of scientists for our country. In 1975, three percent of all the National Merit Scholars sought a major in science education. Last year, less than one percent of the National Merit Scholars sought a career in science education, and this percentage was declining. In the last ten years alone, undergraduate science majors at all universities and colleges in this country have declined 33 percent. One-twentieth of the students in our colleges and universities major in science today, whereas in the late 1960's one-tenth of the students majored in the sciences.

Even the best research universities are affected. The National Academy of Science has chosen the twenty public and private universities with the most notable programs in science education in the country. It has studied those twenty institutions and discovered that last year they conferred fourteen percent fewer degrees than they did in 1980.

What does all this mean? How will it affect us at DePauw? What are the opportunities? You will remember that in the 1960's and 70's, enrollments were high in colleges and significant numbers of faculty were added. But these people will begin retiring in the early- to mid-1990's. By the mid-1990's, the number of Ph.D's will fall off rapidly due to the "baby bust." In short, we are not producing enough scientists in this country to meet our needs. The Oberlin study points out that some liberal arts colleges should be positioned well to reemphasize what we have done well for years, and that is help with the undergraduate production of people interested in science, people who will go on to earn their Ph.D's. The Oberlin Conference showed that graduates of the Oberlin Conference colleges go on to earn doctorates in a significantly higher percentage than do the graduates of either Ivy League schools or the top twenty rated research universities. Last year, the University of Illinois, for instance, produced more Ph.D's in chemistry than they did undergraduate majors in chemistry.

The primary distinction the Oberlin Conference pointed out was that personalized instruction – the kind of instruction we profess at DePauw – by senior faculty with their widespread involvement in the lives of students through research projects has caused these colleges to produce an extraordinarily high percentage of this country's scientists.

So what might we think about this? It seems to me it's something we need to examine carefully. Science education has a strong tradition here. Currently, there is a national concern about science education throughout the country. DePauw should be in the position to be on the vanguard of the developments that will produce more professional scientists in this country.

III.

I want to raise a third opportunity for DePauw or, perhaps if not an opportunity, a third set of questions. I refer to the issue of moral reflection in our community.

The church-related liberal arts college represents a tradition where education and values have traditionally co-existed. We need to ask ourselves if current graduates of DePauw are inculcated with a set of values that will serve beyond the DePauw experience. Do our graduates leave with a sense of divine discontent about injustice in this world? Are they graduated with a coherent frame of reference, a value system if you please, that will serve as a basis for future decisions and actions?

I have been much impressed with DePauw Emeritus Professor Clifton Philips' comments about the history of DePauw and how secularization has affected the institution. In 1904, the DePauw catalogue stated that the Bible was the unquestioned authority on moral issues. By the 1940's, the catalogue simply stated that DePauw had a close relationship with the Methodist Church. In the 1950's, the term used was that DePauw was a "church-related" college, and we expressed our church relatedness with a religious emphasis week – a week we set aside one time a year to renew our historic connections with the Christian faith.

In the 1960's, the Chaplain's Office was created. Earlier, I am told, the President had been the Chaplain.

By the 1980's, instead of any reference to the United Methodist Church, the Bible, or church-relatedness, we simply stated that we emphasized the Judeo-Christian tradition. We no longer taught a course in Christian evidences, but our introductory courses encompassed all world religions.

This experience is not peculiar to DePauw, and it is not one we should lament. In fact, perhaps we should celebrate our movement away from some of the narrow sect-type thinking that permeates many of today's so-called Christian institutions. However, we must wonder if we have given up the concept of moral reflection at a time when students need direction most of all.

The knowledge traditionally taken for granted as being provided by the home, school and church is rarely in evidence today. Students arrive at DePauw as freshmen, knowing little about the facts and ideas that comprise much of our repertoire of basic value information. Our students no longer know about the major prophets, the minor prophets, the teachings of Jesus, the content of the Koran, not to mention the basic tenets of Judaism. Nor do they remember the experiences of Vietnam or Watergate, and their memories of John. F. Kennedy are non-existent.

Let me be very clear. I do not think that colleges should impose values on students. Nor am I proposing that we return to our roots and agree on all the values we are to "pass on." However I do raise the issue of whether our students should not be familiar with the traditions out of which value questions are raised. Should our students not critically examine how values are formed and how they become operative in a society?

We need again to inform our students that values are more than matters of personal taste or private intuition. We are reaching a time when private liberal arts colleges can no longer neglect the value questions so central to our tradition. Consider some of the issues our students will have to face in their lifetime.

Now that medical technology has enabled transplants to become a reality, who will pay the extravagant medical costs of heart transplants, kidney transplants, dialysis, etc., etc.? Who will answer the question raised in the June 9 issue of *The Wall Street Journal* concerning when life-support systems should be withheld? What about abortion these days? After all the debate, has this become simply a private issue?

Since the best of medical care cannot be funded for the entire citizenry, what level of medical care should be guaranteed to everyone? Are there classes of people, by class or education, who shall be denied the best of medical care? If the public cannot afford medical technology for all, who gets it? Only the rich?

Need we not also reflect on genetic engineering? Dare we argue that we have enough basic knowledge of science to even discuss the implications of genetic engineering?

Have we divorced ourselves from the discussion of values in society to the point that Robert Bellah's argument is correct when he says, "The University is no longer the place for the training of leadership in public service in a free society. The University as presently organized isn't set up to engage in public dialogue that would provide moral leadership or even encourage it?" Dare we not provide moral leadership? Dare we not encourage the public dialogue surrounding the issues I have raised?

In the preamble to the Carleton College catalogue you'll find the words that Carleton fosters, "personal and social responsibility as well as academic excellence." Dare we at DePauw do less?

IV.

Diversity, science education, moral reflection – three issues which are in keeping with the traditions of this great University.

But faculty share one enormous problem – time. The Faculty Development Committee has been in discussions with the University Priorities Committee for over one year, trying to allocate time in a more efficient manner. The faculty has spoken and we have heard that the way to make improvements in the intellectual life of our community hinges around a larger and more encompassing faculty development program than we have ever experienced at this University. We need to follow the examples of other premier institutions in this regard. Brown University, for example, upon becoming concerned about the lack of diversity in its curriculum and in its student body, offered incentive grants to faculty for the creation of courses which dealt with multi-ethnic and non-Western cultural diversity. Special support was given to interested members of the faculty to rework existing courses to include more culturally diverse materials. Special support was also used to increase the number of departmental courses which focused on the experience and heritage of the various minority groups so rapidly growing in American society.

Such a faculty development program is imperative for DePauw. We want to become an institution more national and international in scope, but we also have come to realize this is not a public relations task. It is a faculty development task. The faculty needs more time to release from classes to pursue research and course development. We need to consider implementation of incentive awards for travel, and the possibility of an active summer research program.

We are at an interesting point in the institution's history. We are completing the largest campaign ever attempted by a liberal arts college. Our faculty will prove that as resources are made increasingly available to us we are indeed a gathering of insightful minds wanting to better prepare our students for living in the world community. The possibilities are enormous.

In the May 14 issue of *The New York Times*, there was a description of the Committee on Interpretation that grew up at Bryn Mawr College. It began simply as a gathering of faculty across disciplinary lines which met to discuss common educational interests. "These meetings began to chip away at a rather narrow departmental system," said Stephen Levine, Art Historian, "a new intellectual atmosphere resulted."

The evaluation of the Bush Program for Faculty Development at liberal arts colleges in the Midwest contained the following insight: "In a small liberal arts college it is surprising to hear faculty remarking about knowing so little about what other faculty are doing and of not enjoying the relationship with colleagues outside the department."

David Porter began a summer seminar in 1982 at Carleton College which had as its goal the simple task of becoming aware of what other faculty were doing. Twelve to fifteen faculty met together from many disciplines and simply examined the introductory courses that were being taught on the Carleton campus. Porter was quoted as saying, "It was one of the most effective curricular and faculty development strategies ever begun at Carleton."

Such phenomena can come into being at DePauw. In the last week, I have had discussions with Professor Sedlack of the English Department who spoke in convocation about the moral perspective on abortion; with Lisa Wichser, an economics professor who is teaching Chinese as a half-unit course in the evening; and Shanker Shetty, another economics professor who began his efforts to learn the Japanese language at Indiana University this summer. The resources and the creativity among us are great. We need to emulate and further enhance the finest faculty development programs in higher education. Then we can sustain ourselves as the first-rate faculty we know we are.

In his book *American Professors: A National Resource Imperiled,* Harold Bowen speaks out: "The situation today is much like the Sputnik era of thirty years ago – It is underfunded at a time when the educational needs of the nation are enormous."

As a result of the Sesquicentennial Campaign we have the resources to add new faculty to our community. However, before we rush into dividing up these faculty additions among the various departments, let us take care to first examine the needs of the people already in our community. We have a start. With the resources available through the generous endowment established by John and Janice Fisher, and with the institutional funds already being expended on faculty development, we have the ambitious beginnings of a faculty development program longed for at only the most distinguished institutions. We have the opportunity to fund what Bowen calls "in-between research," research that may not be earth shattering in terms of new discoveries coming forth from Greencastle, Indiana, but research that is valuable, not only on its face as an important contribution to a field but is also a vehicle to keep abreast and to continue throughout our lives to be learned men and women and share in the joy of discovery.

V.

Finally, this evening, I want to conclude my address to you with another set of questions. We will definitely answer these questions in the next few years.

Are we ready to become the institution we have the potential to be?

Are we ready to expose our students, our faculty, and our curriculum to the diversity demanded by the world community?

Are we willing to dedicate ourselves to science education and remain one of the forty-seven Oberlin Conference Colleges which have had such an impact on science education in this country?

Are we willing to take again the challenge of the DePauw tradition and assist our students in becoming morally sensitive and keenly aware of the issues of justice, honesty, peace?

If we answer these questions in the affirmative, we do face some problems. Our creativity will be challenged. It will be, for some of us, a lot of trouble. There will be no time for pettiness, for narrow departmentalism, for inward quarreling, and we will have no time to treat each other in any manner other than with civility and respect. Yet if we choose to capitalize on our opportunities, the rewards are tremendous.

We are now poised to take our place among America's finest colleges. We must work together toward that end – not by clinging to the past, but by innovatively moving to the forefront of undergraduate education.

This is an exciting time. From our faculty and administration, we say to the Trustees – For your leadership in the Sesquicentennial campaign which is providing us resources to dream our dreams and implement our visions, we offer a sincere thank you.

And finally, from the administration and the Trustees to the faculty – We thank you for maintaining the high scholarly standards of this institution, and for continuing to challenge our students as alumni have been challenged for generations.

As for myself, I need to thank both the Trustees and the faculty for the high privilege of working with you.

Thank you.

APPENDIX III

"REMARKS BY DR. BOTTOMS AT CAMPUS CONVOCATION ON RACE RELATIONS"

October 19, 1988

W E HAVE EACH IN OUR OWN WAY ALREADY DISCUSSED THE HEALING WHICH NEEDS TO TAKE PLACE. But for true healing to take place, we must first admit that something is potentially very wrong in our community. And to improve our community, it seems to me, we must start with a common understanding among us all.

What happened last Friday evening was <u>wrong</u>. It was wrong for many reasons. Most simply put, it was wrong for us to treat others the way some of our students were treated. Actions that degrade other human beings are wrong. It was also wrong for some of us to feel that because we did not contribute directly to the degradations that we are not responsible for the actions of the community. The actions of last Friday betray the essence of a quality university community. Knowledge in its most pure and enlightened form represents truth and justice and compassion. It is opposed to all behavior that breaks or cripples the human spirit. As we all are coming to realize, last Friday evening does illustrate that somehow this message has not been transmitted very well throughout our whole community.

In the days since last weekend, what have we learned about

ourselves? We have learned that injustice is still present in our society. Not in some far-off, abstract way, but right here in our midst. And I trust we have learned that injustice always hurts people. Secondly, many of us have learned that actions always have consequences. We really should not have been surprised that CBS News, the Associated Press, and *USA Today* paid special attention to us. When something of this nature occurs in a university community people notice. It is not enough to say, "I'm sorry," and go on as if nothing happened. The events of Friday must have some longer-term effects on our lives together.

Where do we go from here? We realize that we cannot make one another moral, nor better. Nor can we make one another behave. We can discipline (and we will), but I also trust we will grow and learn and be made better and stronger by the events of the weekend. I trust we will learn that this road to knowledge will not be an easy path. It will require more than wearing ribbons in support of the minority community. It will require more than conducting convocations like this one. It will require more than our conversations together. In fact, it will even require more than our sorrow, even though I am convinced that we are sorry we hurt our friends. We are sorry we embarrassed the university. And many of us are sorry we did not notice. But the real test is not how sorry we are, but what we can do together to ensure that this will not happen again. If we cannot learn to productively deal with our remorse, the fact is it could happen again.

We have two options. The first is that we pledge together that this will not happen again while we are here. A second and more important option, though, is to see if as a community we find a way to institutionalize our programming and our concern to ensure that these events are not replayed here again. Ever.

We can all strive for excellence in two areas. We can put our own lives in order and we can use them to instruct others. One very traditional goal of the university has been to transmit knowledge and values from one generation to another. I hope we will institutionalize what we learned last Friday and that this knowledge will impact future generations of students. Our goals in this regard are both educational and moral.

As I have discussed with you on other occasions, we simply must learn to live together with respect for others. We have to learn to tolerate and to appreciate differences. The stakes in this educational enterprise are enormous. The stakes are large for us as individuals and the quality of life we will lead after we leave this community. The stakes are large for our college and the kind of community we will continue to have at this university. It is not overly dramatic to say that the stakes in our educational enterprise are also important and have far-reaching implications for our very country. For if we can't learn to live together in a small community of 2,400 students, we will have a difficult time with the world of the 21st century.

Tonight we come together to admit a wrong, to ask forgiveness, and to move beyond defensiveness and name-calling. We have the opportunity to make a covenant that we will earnestly do all in our power to correct wrongs, to grow in understanding, and to work to make the university stronger, more humane, and more inclusive.

In an academic community it is possible for the classroom to form our very interpretation of life, and for our classroom experiences to illuminate and enhance our very being. Along this line I would like to share with you some very famous words that illustrate how our classroom experience can illumine our existence. They are words written in 1963 by Martin Luther King. They are words that you read and discussed during freshman orientation last year, for they are taken from Martin Luther King's "Letter from a Birmingham Jail." He writes, "We will have to repent in this generation not merely for the hateful words and actions of the bad people, but for the appalling silence of the good people. Human progress never rolls on wheels of inevitability. It comes through the tireless efforts of men and women willing to be co-workers with God, and without this hard work time itself becomes an ally of the forces of social stagnation. We must use time creatively and in the knowledge that the time is always ripe to do the right thing."

We gather to say we repent and we are sorry. We gather to say we are beginning the hard work of improving the quality of life in our community. We gather to say we are ready to move beyond our anger and our hurt. We gather to pledge, as King pledged before us, that we will use our time creatively to erase hurt and pain. The time is always right and ripe to do the right thing.

Thank you.

Appendix IV

Two Speeches On Diversity

#1--Speech For Opening Academic Convocation

Saturday, August 24, 1996

Introduction

As I stand here today – to welcome you, the class of 2000 – I want you to know what a humbling experience this is for me.

Like you, I once sat in an academic convocation to open my first-year of college.

Like some of you, I was the first member of my family to attend college.

I was excited…I was nervous.

If it hadn't been for my grandfather's influence, I might not have gone to college.

I never put on this academic robe that I don't think of him.

Of how this poorly-educated, but very bright steel-working man instilled in me at a very early age the desire to go to college.

Like me, some of you have been influenced by others or you wouldn't be here.

Covenant today that you will so use your four years here that those who influenced you will one day be proud as you walk across East College lawn to receive your degree.

Others of you come from families where everyone has gone to college.

If that is the case, as your parents sit here with you today they are probably recalling their first day on campus.

Perhaps the faculty that sits behind me are even thinking about their first few days on campus.

Some of us can even recall the back pain and the perspiration.

However, when my generation moved into college, we moved a footlocker and a suitcase.

You move footlockers, suitcases, sound systems, computers, and all sorts of musical instruments and athletic equipment.

As your families recall their college experiences and think about what they want for you, use your four years here so that they, too, can be proud as you receive your degree.

I. Before we think too much about what your DePauw experience will be, let us first remember those who worked so hard for this University long before any of us came here.

A. I think of the Methodists who founded this University in 1837.

Once the Methodists decided to establish a college in Indiana, a committee was appointed to draw up the charter for the new college.

Another committee was chosen to evaluate the towns competing for the location of the school.

The competition for the location of the college would be based upon three factors:

The amount of money raised

The general state of health of the town

And the general state of the morals of the town

Greencastle raised $25,000 to ensure the selection of the Putnam County seat over towns like Indianapolis, LaFayette, Madison, Rockville, and Putnamville.

In making its case, one of the proud boosters of Greencastle, Dr. Tarvin Cowgill, allegedly said, "People never die in Greencastle, although for convenience they have a cemetery there."

According to the charter established by a second committee, the University was founded for the benefit "of the youth of every class of citizens and every religious denomination, who shall be freely admitted to equal advantages and privileges of education."

The charter refers to an extensive university, "to be conducted on the most liberal principles and accessible to all."

B. The University moved forward in the early days to act upon these principles.

DePauw opened its doors to African-American students

early in its life.

On September 14, 1882, the *Greencastle Banner* reported that George Washington Ziegler, a black pastor of a local Methodist church, had enrolled in the University.

Pointing out that Ziegler was "the first of his race to enter as a student," the local weekly noted that he was "kindly received by both faculty and students."

A month later another African-American student, Tucker Wilson, joined Ziegler.

Tucker Wilson did, in fact, become DePauw's first African-American graduate when he received his degree in June, 1888, and Mr. Wilson was one of 17 members of the 40-member senior class to make a presentation at Commencement.

Today, DePauw has chosen to carry on this tradition of educating minority leadership.

I think Tucker Wilson undoubtedly would be proud of the contemporary DePauw.

C. Just as I think of the Methodists who laid the foundation for this institution, I think of the hundreds of faculty who have taught here for generations.

Take a look at our faculty (They look pretty good.).

In fact, this is about the best we ever look.

The hoods worn by the faculty represent both the schools they attended and the subjects in which they took their doctoral degrees.

Collectively, our faculty has spent over 1,000 years of study to prepare themselves to help you grow over the next four years.

Each person seated behind me on the stage could tell you of faculty who have influenced them, who opened new worlds for them, and they are dedicated to doing the same for you.

D. As I continue to reflect on those who prepared the contemporary DePauw for you, I also think of the thousands of DePauw alumni.

In the last ten years, DePauw alumni have given over $150 million to this institution.

They believe it is a very special place and they want you to use it to enhance your growth.

E. I have more thoughts about the past, but I will move on because I am certain of one thing.

You'll probably never remember very much of what I say.

But I do hope you'll remember this.

I hope you remember the tenor and tone of this convocation.

It is rather formal.

It's our way of saying that what you do here will be very important.

A college education is not to be taken for granted.

Education will not just happen to you.

You have to be an active participant for it to work for you.

F. Education has become the most important investment you will ever make.

It's not just the money that you pay to attend, but it is the investment of your time.

You will be here for four years with proficient faculty.

You have over 150 faculty tutors all dedicated to your intellectual growth.

This is an experience to be coveted.

Pledge yourself to make the most of it.

You have a privilege awaiting you that many in the world will never know.

G. You are part of a great tradition.

One day – in four years – you will receive your degree.

At that time, you will be a different person.

You will stand before this faculty and be admitted to the community of college graduates throughout the world.

If we have done our work well together, you will be a different person.

A person:

More deeply aware of beauty,

More deeply aware of complexity,

Of suffering,

And of truth – than when you entered.

II. How is this education to take place, this process of growth and of change?

What will your DePauw education be like?

    A. Quite simply, your education will supply you with intellectual capital.

    You build this capital by learning from the past,

    developing standards to measure good and bad,

    by being introduced to new ideas.

    You build capital by probing the mysteries of the natural world,

    learning why some cultures failed,

    how others survived.

    You build capital by being awakened to art and music

and the way these forces have expressed peoples' hopes and dreams and nightmares and despairs.

    b. Education is about answering questions and solving

        problems:

        Who am I?

        How do I do this?

        How does this work?

        We want you to learn to question everything while you

are here.

        Develop theories to answer your questions.

        Test these theories.

        Then reflect on what you have learned and continue to

interrogate yourself again

        and again and again.

III. Your education can affect you in two ways: one private and one public.

    A. Let's first look at the education of the private self.

        1. Much of life is spent alone.

        Thinking

        Reading

        Studying

        Working at computers

        Waiting

Quality education teaches you how to be alone, how to value solitude.

2. We often avoid the pleasures of silence.

We turn on stereos.

We turn on televisions.

We make telephone calls.

We see a movie – We fill our times of silence with many noisy things.

Some critics of contemporary society have long declared that we may not know how to be alone, to enjoy quietness as a time of growth.

Perhaps this is because if we are left alone with our thoughts, we discover we have few and that we are not good company for ourselves.

a. Education can address this possibility.

Education equips us to entertain ourselves with ideas.

Often our most creative moments come when we are alone...when we use our education to contemplate novel approaches to our lives.

So as you commit to your education at DePauw, commit yourselves to the education of a private self.

The self that is thirsty to understand.

A self that can find peace in the quiet.

A self that can respond to ideas.

And a self that uniquely uses the tools of learning to grow and constantly be renewed.

B. I trust you will use your education here to define not only your private self, but your public self.

1. I trust you will use your education to become a person of integrity.

When Stephen Carter in his book *Integrity* defined the term, he helpfully stated that integrity requires three steps:

a. Use your education to discern what is right and wrong.

b. Have the courage to <u>act</u> on what you have discerned.

c. Say <u>openly</u> that you are acting on your understanding of right and wrong.

In order to live with integrity, it is sometimes necessary to take that difficult step to get involved – to fight openly for what one believes to be true and right and good even when there is personal risk.

This doesn't mean that you have to fight your way through life.

But it addresses the fact that a number of us seem to be happy to drift through life, activists on behalf of none of our beliefs.

2. If society is to improve, we must as educated people develop a public and involved self.

a. Seven years before DePauw was founded, Alexis de Tocqueville came from France to observe what we Americans were about.

He wrote, "Citizens who are bound to take part in public affairs must turn from private interests and occasionally take a look at something larger than themselves."

de Tocqueville saw Americans doing just that, using their religious commitments and civic associations to publicly involve themselves in improving our country.

b. de Tocqueville is telling us to keep things going, to make things better.

Edmund Burke, in writing about the French Revolution, stated that "Society is indeed a contract…not only between those who are living, but between those who are living…those who are dead…and those who are yet to be born."

Education and an involved public self fulfills our responsibility to those who will come after us as well as our duty to those who will come after us as well as our duty to those who have come before us.

c. It is through our educated public selves that we

become involved in the problems of society.

America has long been known as a land of promise.

We struggle today to live up to those promises – our obligation to immigrants, to racial equity, and gender equity.

DePauw promised in 1837 to be open to all people.

We are just beginning to learn what that means.

DePauw has worked hard in the last ten years to be welcoming to people of all the ethnic backgrounds.

We did this work because before our eyes we have seen America virtually remade.

There is a dramatic increase in the influence of African-Americans, Latino people, Asian-Americans, and other ethnic groups.

Unless we learn as a society to take full advantage of what each group has to offer, America will not fulfill our promise.

Learning to fulfill the potential of all the minority communities in our society is a role for our public selves.

And, Do You Know What?

It is also good for us individuals as we develop our private selves.

It is in persons least like ourselves who often teach us the most…who challenge us to examine what we have always accepted.

As we open our minds to the symphony of different cultures, different traditions and different languages, we have the opportunity to grow not only publicly, but privately.

C. You come to DePauw at a special time.

We have created a laboratory for you to learn how to deal with different people and how to nurture shared bonds.

Some of you come to DePauw without knowledge of people from different races or different economic backgrounds.

But you have the opportunity at DePauw to use your education to genuinely learn about all the people who make up our country.

Our faculty and your readings will help you.

Barbara Kingsolver, DePauw Class of 1977, the noted contemporary author, wrote these words about the influence of books on her understanding of people.

She said, "I know, for example, that slavery was heinous, but the fate of 60 million slaves is too big a thing for a heart to understand."

So it was not until I read Toni Morrison's *Beloved* that I honestly felt that truth.

"When Seth killed her children rather than have them grow up in slavery, I was so far from my sheltered self that I knew the horror that could make infanticide an act of love."

Morrison carved the tragedy of those 60 million slaves, to whom the book is dedicated, into something small and dense and real enough to fit through the door, get in my heart and explode.

This is how a novel can be more true than a newspaper.

My friend Johnetta Cole, president of Spelman College, in her commencement address at Emory University last spring commented on the task that is before us if we are able to see the full potential of all races in the country.

Dr. Cole evoked a passage from the Gospel of Mark, words echoed by Abraham Lincoln in 1858, to set the theme for her address.

"And if a house be divided against itself, that house cannot stand."

The problem is that in this house of ours, we have not yet found a way to teach people how to decently and lovingly interact with those who are different. We have not yet proven to the satisfaction of all, the power of people engaging across communities to solve problems.

Cole gleaned lessons from Anthropology, her field of expertise, for reuniting what she called "our divided house… each of you not matter what career you are about to engage in must surely lend a hand in rebuilding and fortifying our house."

That is what is meant by the public self.

Conclusion

One of the first addresses many of our students have heard in the past few years was the commencement address given by Cornel West of Harvard University at DePauw last spring.

In his address Cornel reminded us that while the tasks before us are great, not one of us is a messiah.

We will not save ourselves.

We will not save America.

We will not save the world.

But we can certainly leave it just a little bit better than we found it.

The future we predict today is not inevitable.

We can influence it if we know what we want it to be.

If you, as the entering class, believe that the world is incomplete and that history is unfinished and that the future is open-ended, what you do and what you think in the next four years will make a difference.

Thank you.

2 – "OPENING CONVOCATION"
SATURDAY, AUGUST 23, 1997
3:30 PM, KRESGE AUDITORIUM

Introduction

WE ARE PLEASED TO SEE ALL OF YOU HERE. It has been a good day…We have had nice weather…All the students have "sort of" moved in…And the faculty looks very good today. In fact, this may be the very best you will see them look until next year's commencement. The hoods they wear – with the bright colors – represent the various areas of academic specialty. Also, the colors surrounding their hoods represent the institutions from which they were graduated.

While any high-quality college faculty represents many divergent philosophies, the DePauw faculty is united by two factors:

1) They are experts in their field.

and,

2) They want to offer you the opportunity for a liberal arts education.

According to our charter, in 1837 DePauw University was founded for your benefit – the youth of every class of citizen. We are, in the words of our charter "to conduct ourselves on the most liberal principles and benefit of our country."

When our founders wrote these words 160 years ago, little did they know what a truly significant institution DePauw would become. Today I want to illustrate for you how the charter of 1837 still guides us – how we liberally educate students, and how we hope to prepare good citizens.

For many generations, DePauw has held certain core values. We are an undergraduate institution. We are small in size. We teach the liberal arts. We hope to graduate morally-sensitive students. These values have not changed in over 160 years.

Given these constant core values, how shall we describe the contemporary DePauw? In other words, how will we relate to one another for the next four years? We will read and write and talk and reason together. We will learn different languages. We will encounter people from different backgrounds. We are basically bright people. We are ethnically-diverse and economically-diverse. Some of us know what we want to do with our lives and some of us do not. Some of us are confident and some of us are scared.

To be sure, we come in all sizes and colors. But we should have one thing in common: we seek the <u>opportunity</u> to grow intellectually, and to pursue those liberal – and liberating – principles our founders wrote about.

At the most fundamental level, we have invited you to Greencastle to help you arrange your lives. As you move through your four years at DePauw, many of your experiences will be planned by us, but some of them will be serendipitous. Along the way you will be challenged, surprised, dismayed, amused, baffled, excited, disturbed...and affirmed. We trust that out of these experiences you will grow in maturity and develop the ability to act intelligently.

I. Think with me further about the purpose of your DePauw education.

Many of us would contend that the liberal arts teach you to think. But thinking is automatic. You think all the time. What we really want to do is to have you think in better ways.

We also say we want to teach you to think independently, to think for yourselves. To think for yourself does not mean we want you to think as differently as possible. People who are insane do that. Instead we want you to master a body of knowledge that represents a mutual understanding of learned people everywhere.

Developing good habits of mind...learning to think independently...to think critically...these are not the traits the public often associates with college. The public seems to believe in the pegboard view of education. According to this view, the outside world is like a giant board consisting of an array of differently-shaped job slots. The role of college then becomes to produce the right-shaped people, the pegs, who will fill these slots. This is not what we are about at DePauw.

Here we believe it is more important to know <u>who you are than where you are going</u>, for the latter will change as the world does. In fact, if you are a typical graduate you will have not one, but several, jobs in your career. Who you are is more important than what you do.

Society holds many definitions of who you are, and quite frankly, some of these answers are better than others. Deep down you already know that some answers are better than others. If you didn't know this, you would not argue with your parents and friends about what you think, as opposed to what they might think. You defend your opinions and you do not behave as if the differing opinions about life are just matters of taste. Your willingness to attempt to justify your own position about who you are implies that you know that there are better and worse answers to the all-important questions:

How should you live?

and,

What should you believe in?

We have many tools for you, to assist in helping you define yourselves. We call these tools readings and tests and research papers. But twenty years from now, if truth be told, you may remember altogether very little about the <u>particulars</u> of what this faculty will teach you during your four years here. I call this Educational Amnesia. But, even though in 20 years many of the facts you learn here will be forgotten, you will come to realize that this experience of college changed your life. For at DePauw you will have encountered teachers who not only befriended you, but forced you to admit that there were important questions for which your answers were inadequate. You will have been introduced to great books by significant teachers, from whom in later years you can draw sustenance. All faculty on stage have students who so come alive by reading some books that students continue to read and re-read. If you become like other alumni, you will make deep and lifelong relationships at DePauw, friendships based in large measure on sharing conversations with faculty and students – sometimes in class, sometimes not – the attempt to understand the experience of the world and your own humanity.

Some people have compared college to a base camp used by mountain climbers. The way the story goes is simple. If you want to climb a mountain, you develop a good base camp, a place where there is shelter and where provisions are kept, a place where you can rest before you venture our again to seek another summit. Successful mountain climbers know they must spend as much time tending to their base camp as they actually do in climbing mountains, for their survival is dependent upon their seeing to it that their base camp is sturdily-constructed and well-stocked. A liberal arts education is a wonderful base camp for venturing out into life.

Point One: Use you DePauw Education as a Base Camp for the Rest of your Life.

II. Point Two: How will you use what you learn here? I hope you will use your education in the service of others.

Educators have known for decades that learning is social. Perhaps one of the most significant opportunities we offer to enhance out-of-class learning is DePauw's Volunteer Service Program. Here you have the opportunity to learn to work in teams, to work as male and female, and to work with people from different ethic backgrounds. These experiences of working together with a variety of people to solve common problems will complement your classroom education.

At DePauw our Community Service Programs are perhaps our best example of teaching citizenship. Most college mission statements mention citizenship, but it is highly questionable if many colleges actually do much to develop citizenship in students. This is exactly what DePauw attempts to do through community service.

By learning citizenship we mean building the elements of character that lead to ethical actions…traits like autonomy, respecting the dignity of others, compassion, kindness, honesty, and commitment to equity and fairness.

The college years have a profound impact on moral character, and community service helps you think about yourself in relation to others. Who are your neighbors, and what are your obligations to them?

And, you know what? Community Service – working with students in grade schools or older people in nursing homes – strengthens academic learning. Alexander Astin of UCLA conducted a national survey, using 35 different outcome measures covering the areas of academic development, civic values, and life skills. What was especially remarkable about the findings is that every one of the 35 student outcomes was positively-influenced by student service participation.

Through the Community Service Program at DePauw you will learn that your life can make a difference. We do not have to believe that we have no influence in the world. At DePauw we focus on the scale where we think we can have influence, and we practice the traits of citizenship that will later allow us to tackle the larger problems of the world outside DePauw. Your DePauw education will make a difference if it is used with the intention to serve people.

George Bernard Shaw said, "This is the true joy of life…being used for a [mighty] purpose…being a force instead of a feverish, selfish little clod of ailments and grievances, complaining that the world will not devote itself to making you happy."

I hope while you are at DePauw you will use the opportunities provided you as a chance to become involved and to learn that your education can benefit society…and can be used to solve problems.

III. *The third point I want to discuss deals with the diversity you will encounter in the DePauw community.*

DePauw is amazingly like the society you will confront after graduating from the University. We are well-off and we are poor. We are Black, White, Asian, Hispanic, and mixed. We are male and female. We are gay and straight. We truly are a laboratory in which we can learn how to develop as individuals.

At DePauw we have built a diverse community of students and faculty to enhance the responsibility of learning from one another and to prepare us to function in contemporary America.

Why do I say this? Our country is experiencing a dramatic change in the composition of the population. Between 2000 and 2010, forty percent of new entrants into the labor force will be minorities. We want DePauw graduates to be able to effectively navigate in a society more ethnically-diverse than America has ever known.

After graduation you will find yourselves responsible for facilitating the performance of racially-diverse groups. People with limited experience of working with different peoples will be intimidated. We do not want this to happen to you, whether you

are African-American, White, Asian or Latino. A contemporary
DePauw experience should allow you to be at ease with different
ethic groups – at ease, in fact, because you had four years of
practice right here in Greencastle.

I want to highlight this notion of diversity in a simple way.
Visualize a jar of <u>red</u> jellybeans. Now imagine adding some <u>green</u>
and <u>purple</u> jellybeans. Some would believe that the green and
purple jellybeans represent diversity. I suggest that diversity
instead is represented by the result of the <u>mixture</u> of red, green and
purple jellybeans.

When faced with a collection of diverse jellybeans, most
people worry about how to handle the last jellybeans added to
the mixture…the green and purple ones. This is not dealing with
diversity. The person who is truly coping with racial diversity is
not dealing with Blacks, Whites, Latinos, or Asian Americans, but
rather with the collective mixture. In other words, the mixture is
all-inclusive, and each part has an effect on all other parts.

In dealing with difference, we move along a continuum
from intolerance to mutual enhancement. We first must learn to
tolerate those who are different. We can then move to accepting
the differences (housing and barbecues). We can then move to
appreciate the art, dance, and music of different cultures. However,
few of us experience the highest potential of living in a diverse
community – the move to mutual enhancement, where each

group is elevated by the other and we learn to solve our problems together.

It is important to realize that no one group gets it all right, no single person, no single culture. Any group can be enhanced by the other.

At DePauw the classroom and the campus are contact zones. These are places of intersection, all places where we bump up against each other. We will negotiate how it is that we will live with one another.

In an article in *Change* magazine, Martin Nagy states:

There was once, so Schopenhauer tells us, a colony of porcupines. They wanted to huddle together on a cold winter's day and, thus wrapped in communal warmth, escape being frozen. But, plagued with the pricks of each others' quills, they drew apart. And every time the desire for warmth brought them together again. The same calamity overtook them. Thus they remained, able neither to tolerate one another nor to do without one another, until they discovered that when they stood at a certain distance from one another, they could both delight in one another's individuality and enjoy one another's company. Unknown to themselves, they had invented civil association.

The porcupines learned to position themselves at "a certain distance" from each other. Those who wandered off on a cold night might freeze to death, and certainly could not contribute to the common good. Those who huddled too close on the same night…were "plagued with the pricks of each other's quills."

We are realistic in knowing that our efforts to achieve community among all the different groups are, at times, a source of a certain prickliness. Yet our goals should be not to eliminate those tensions by abandoning our efforts for mutual enhancement, but rather to embrace tensions and to engage them to build a richer understanding of others.

And, do you know what? Researchers tell us that diversity has the same positive effect on the classroom as does community service. Darryl Smith, a Professor of Education at Claremont Graduate School, has pointed out that when campuses are diverse, students actually learn more. When we are involved in a classroom conversation about something that is important and we have multiple perspectives addressing it, critical thinking improves.

An example might be useful. We need to think about the issues of diversity in the same way we think about technology. Recall ten or fifteen years ago, when our campuses acknowledged that we were living in a technological society. The response on our campuses then was, "We can't have our students going out there unprepared to deal with technology."

If a student has not experience with technology or is frightened by it, we do not say, "Don't worry about it." We work very hard to engage that student. The same has to be true with diversity. We have to work hard to engage our students with faculty and students who are "different." We should never say, "Don't worry about it." Instead, we'd say, "Why don't we learn to deal with it?"

Our diversity challenges every DePauw student and faculty member and administrator to try to understand the values and memories of each community represented here, to hear the voices of the powerless and the powerful, and everyone in between, with equal resonance...and to understand that we belong to multiple communities at one time.

Conclusion

I have talked about the value of a DePauw education, the value of service, and the value of living in a diverse community. Now the responsibility is yours. You may fulfill that responsibility through your classes, your Winter Term experiences, through your service opportunities. If you live up to your potential you can grow, but there is also a dark side...you can also live in such a way as to not take advantage of the opportunities we offer. Then DePauw can be disappointing. It is really left to you and how responsible for your own education you become.

As a DePauw students, don't cheat yourself by just seeking to get by. Your four years here will not sustain you in later life, not provide that base camp, if you are willing to be satisfied with mediocrity.

A DePauw education requires participation. You cannot watch it happen. You have to do it.

In closing, let me express my hopes for you, the DePauw Class of 2001.

I wish for you an immersion in education. I hope you find DePauw a place where the spirit of critique <u>and</u> civility co-exist passionately.

I wish for you the development of your intellect, made possible by the rigor of your daily work.

I hope you discover the joys of service to others.

I wish for you the knowledge that, no matter how different, everyone counts.

I wish for you the ability to imagine with accuracy just how the world might look and feel to those different from you.

And finally, I wish for you the ability to develop your own eccentricities – your class possesses many unique individuals – let's don't all try to be alike.

Welcome to DePauw. Find great enjoyment in the community we've invited you to join.

Thank you.

Appendix V

Ubben Lecturers

Heads of State

Willy Brandt – Former Chancellor of West Germany and Nobel Peace Prize Winner

Benazir Bhutto – Former Prime Minister of Pakistan

Shimon Peres – Former Prime Minister of Israel

Margaret Thatcher – Former Prime Minister of Great Britain

John Major – Former Prime Minister of Great Britain

Tony Blair – Former Prime Minister of Great Britain

Brian Mulroney – Former Prime Minister of Canada

Mikhail Gorbachev – Former Soviet Leader and Nobel Prize Winner

Politicians

Zbigniew Brzezinski – Former National Security Advisor

William Bennett – Former Secretary of Education

Paul Tsongas – Presidential Candidate

Lynne Cheney – Former Chair, The National Endowment for the Humanities

General Colin Powell – Former Secretary of State

Barbara Bush – Former First Lady

H. Ross Perot – Presidential Candidate

Bill Bradley – Former United States Senator

Alan Simpson – Retired United States Senator

Robert Gates – Former Director of the CIA

General Wesley Clark – Former Presidential Candidate

Richard Luger – Former United States Senator

Ambassador Paul Bremer III – Envoy to Iraq

William S. Cohen – Former Secretary of Defense

Ralph Nader – Former Presidential Candidate

David Plouffe – Obama's 2008 Campaign Advisor

Civil Rights Leaders
Mary Frances Berry – Historian

Reverend Jesse Jackson – Former Presidential Candidate

Roger Wilkins – Educator

Julian Bond – Activist

Andrew Young – Former Ambassador to the United Nations

Harry Belafonte – Activist

Spike Lee – Producer and Movie Director

Authors
Alan Bloom – Philosopher

Elie Wiesel – Nobel Prize Winner

Lester Thurow – Economist

Sister Helen Prejean – Anti-prison Activist

Christopher Edley, Jr. – Senior Advisor to President Clinton

Jonathan Kozol – Activist

Seymour Hersh – Pulitzer Prize Winner

Doris Kearns Goodwin – Pulitzer Prize Winning Historian

David McCullough – Pulitzer Prize Winning Historian

Eric Schlosser

Mitch Albom

Charles Fishman

Naomi Wolf

Greg Mortenson

Representatives of the Press
Tom Wicker – Former *New York Times* Columnist

Carl Rowan – Journalist

David Broder – Pulitzer Prize Winner

Allen "Al" Neuharth – Founder, *USA Today*

George Will – Pulitzer Prize Winner

Ken Burns – Award-Winning documentary filmmaker

Bob Woodward – Pulitzer Prize Winner

Gwen Ifill – NBC News

Gloria Borger – *US News and World Report*

Sam Donaldson – ABC News

David Gergen – Journalist

Various
James Lovell – Astronaut and Apollo 13 Commander

Dr. David Ho – AIDS Researcher and 1996 Time Magazine Man of the Year

Ferid Murad – 1998 Nobel Laureate in Medicine

Mike Krzyzewski – Basketball Coach, Duke University

Ben Cohen and Jerry Greenfield – Founders of "Ben and Jerry's" Ice Cream

Paul Volcker – Former Chair of the Federal Reserve

E.O. Wilson – Biologist and Pulitzer Prize Winning Author

Paul Rusesabagina – Real-life hero of *Hotel Rwanda*

Liz Murray – "Homeless to Harvard: The Liz Murray Story," made-for-TV movie

Peyton Manning – Football player

Jim Ailing – President of Starbucks, USA

BIBLIOGRAPHY

Armstrong, Karen, *The Case for God*. Canada: Alfred A. Knopf, 2009

_____, *Twelve Steps to a Compassionate Life*. Canada: Alfred A. Knopf, 2010

Badaracco, Joseph L., Jr. *Defining Moments*. Printed in the United States: Harvard Business School Press, 1997

Borg, Marcus J. *Meeting Jesus for the First Time*. Printed in the United States: HarperCollins, 1994

_____, *The Heart of Christianity*. Printed in the United States: HarperCollins, 2003

_____, *Speaking Christian*. Printed in the United States: HarperCollins, 2014

_____, *Convictions*. Printed in the United States: HarperCollins, 2014

Bottoms, Robert, *The Practical Implications of Paul Tillich's Theology For a Doctrine of Church Renewal*. Nashville, Tennessee: Vanderbilt University, 1972

Brooks, David, *The Road to Character*. New York: Random House, 2015

_____, *The Second Mountain*. New York: Random House, 2015

Brown, Brene, *Rising Strong*. New York: Spiegel and Grau, 2015

Brown, Mackensie D., *Ultimate Concern: Tillich in Dialogue*. Printed in the United States: Harper and Row, 1965

Cone, James H., *The Cross and the Lynching Tree*. Maryknoll, NY: Orbis Books, 2011

_____, *Said I Wasn't Gonna Tell Nobody*. Maryknoll, NY: Orbis Books, 2018

Cox, Harvey, *When Jesus Came to Harvard*. New York: Houghton

Mifflin Company, 2006

Douglas, Kelly Brown, *Stand Your Ground*. Maryknoll, NY: Orbis Books, 2015

Edmundson, Mark, *Self and Soul*. Printed in the United States: President and Fellow of Harvard College, 2015

Felten, David M. and Proctor-Murphy, Jeff, *Living the Questions*. New York: HarperCollins, 2012

Franklin, Robert Michael, *Moral Leadership*. Maryknoll, NY: Orbis Books, 2020

George, Bill, *True North*. San Francisco: Josey-Bass, 2007

Goleman, Daniel, *Emotional Intelligence*. Printed in the United States: Bantam Books, 1995

_____, *Focus*. Printed in the United States: Bantam Books, 1995

Goodwin, Doris Kearns, *Leadership in Turbulent Times*. New York: Simon and Schuster, 2018

Harvard Business Review, On Managing Yourself. Printed in the United States: Harvard Business School Corporation, 2010

Heath, Chip and Heath, Dan, *Decisive*. Printed in the United States: Crown Business, 2010

Hollaway, Richard, *Leaving Alexandria*. Published in Great Britain: Canongate Books, 2012

Johnson, Dale A. (Editor), *Vanderbilt Divinity School*. Printed in the United States: Vanderbilt University Press, 2001

Jones, Serene, *Call it Grace*. Printed in the United States: Penguin Random House LLC, 2019

Kluge, P.F., *Alma Mater*. New York: Addison-Wesley Publishing Company, 1993

Kraemer, Harry M. Jansen, Jr., *From Values to Action*. San Francisco: Josey-Bass, 2011

Krattenmaker, Tom, *Confessions of a Secular Jesus Follower*. Printed in the United States: Convergent Books, 2016

Laney, James T., *The Education of the Heart*. Printed in the United States: Emory University, 1994

Lewis, Harry R., *Excellence Without Soul*. Printed in the United States: Perseus Books Group, 2006

McLaren, Brian D., *Why Did Jesus, Moses, the Buddha and Mohammed Cross the Road?* New York: Jericho Books, 2012

Manhart, George B., *DePauw Through the Years: Volumes One and Two*. Greencastle, Indiana: DePauw University, 1962

Mother Teresa, *Come Be My Light*. New York: Doubleday Religion, 2007

Neiman, Susan, *Moral Clarity*. Orlando: Harcourt Books, 2008

Pagels, Elaine, *Why Religion?* Printed in the United States: HarperCollins, 2018

Phillips, Clifton J. and Baughman, John J., *DePauw A Practical History*. Greencastle, Indiana: DePauw University, 1987

Sandel, Michael, *Justice*. New York: Farrar, Straus and Giroux, 2009

Schweitzer, Albert, *The Quest of the Historical Jesus*. London: Adam and Charles Black, 1911

Spong, John Shelby, *Jesus for the Non-Religious*. Printed in the United States: HarperCollins, 2007

_____, *Unbelievable*. Printed in the United States: HarperCollins, 2018

Tillich, Hannah, *From Time to Time*. New York: Stein and Day, 1973

Tillich, Paul, *Systematic Theology Volumes I-III*. Chicago: The University of Chicago Press, Volume I, 1951, Volume II, 1957, Volume III, 1963

_____, *The Courage To Be*. Printed in the United States: Yale University Press, 1952

_____, *The New Being*. Printed in the United States: Charles Scribner's Sons, 1955

_____, *The Shaking of Foundations*. Printed in the United States: Charles Scribner's Sons, 1948

Wright, Robert, *Moral Animals*. Published in the United States: Vintage Books, 1994